Beyond Jennifer & Jason

By the Same Authors

Beyond Charles & Diana:
  An Anglophile's Guide to Baby Naming
Beyond Sarah & Sam:
  An Enlightened Guide to Jewish Baby Naming
Beyond Shannon & Sean:
  An Enlightened Guide to Irish Baby Naming

BEYOND
JENNIFER
&
JASON

An Enlightened Guide to Naming Your Baby

LINDA ROSENKRANTZ & PAMELA REDMOND SATRAN

St. Martin's Press
New York

Excerpt from *Wilderness Tips* by Margaret Atwood. Copyright © 1991 by O.W. Toad Limited. Used by permission of Doubleday, a Division of Bantam Doubleday Dell Publishing Group, Inc.

Excerpt from *Talking It Over* by Julian Barnes. Copyright © 1991 by Julian Barnes. Used by permission of Alfred A. Knopf, Inc., a Division of Random House Inc.

Excerpt from *Mayflower Madam* by Sydney Biddle Barrows and William Novak. Copyright © 1986 by Sydney Barrows and William Novak. Used by permission of William Morrow & Company, Inc.

Excerpt from *Family and Friends* by Anita Brookner. Copyright © 1985 by Anita Brookner. Reprinted by permission of Pantheon Books Inc., a Division of Random House Inc.

Excerpt from *Latecomers* by Anita Brookner. Copyright © 1989 by Anita Brookner. Reprinted by permission of Pantheon Books Inc., a Division of Random House Inc.

Excerpt from *Henry James: The Untried Years* by Leon Edel. Copyright © 1953 by Leon Edel. Copyright renewed. Used by permission of Harper-Collins Publishers, Inc.

Excerpt from *If You Can't Live Without Me, Why Aren't You Dead Yet?* by Cynthia Heimel. Copyright © 1991 by Cynthia Heimel. Used by permission of Grove/Atlantic Monthly Press.

Excerpt from *Almost Paradise* by Susan Isaacs. Copyright © 1984 by Susan Isaacs. Used by permission of HarperCollins Publishers, Inc.

Excerpt from *Song of Solomon* by Toni Morrison. Copyright © 1977 by Toni Morrison. Used by permission of International Creative Management, Inc.

Excerpt from *Darcy's Utopia* by Fay Weldon. Copyright © 1990 by Fay Weldon. Used by permission of Viking Penguin, a division of Penguin Books USA Inc.

BEYOND JENNIFER & JASON Copyright © 1988, 1990, 1994 by Linda Rosenkrantz and Pamela Redmond Satran. All rights reserved. Printed in the United States of America. No part of this book may be used or reproduced in any manner whatsoever without written permission except in the case of brief quotations embodied in critical articles or reviews. For information, address St. Martin's Press, 175 Fifth Avenue, New York, N.Y. 10010.

Library of Congress Cataloging-in-Publication Data
Rosenkrantz, Linda.
  Beyond Jennifer and Jason / Linda Rosenkrantz. — 2nd rev. ed.
    p.   cm.
  ISBN: 0-312-10426-X (pbk.)
    1. Names, Personal—United States.   I. Satran, Pamela Redmond.
II. Title.
CS2377.R67   1994
929.4′4′0973—dc20   93-42666

10 9 8 7 6 5

For our wonderful daughters
Chloe Samantha Finch
and
Rory Elizabeth Margaret Satran

ABOUT THE AUTHORS

LINDA ROSENKRANTZ is the author of the novel *Talk* and co-author of *Gone Hollywood* and *SoHo*. The former editor of *Auction* magazine, she now writes a nationally syndicated column on collectibles. She currently lives in Los Angeles with her husband and daughter.

PAMELA REDMOND SATRAN is a columnist for *Parenting* magazine and also writes a syndicated newspaper column on working parenthood. Her essays and articles appear frequently in *Working Mother, Glamour, Redbook*, and other national magazines. She is the author of a book on style and a novel, and lives in New Jersey with her husband and three children.

Together, the authors have written a series of books on British names, Irish names, and Jewish names.

CONTENTS

ACKNOWLEDGMENTS

Our first thanks go to our editor, Hope Dellon, for believing in this project and for bringing it to its perfect realization. Special thanks to Nancy Fish for her early input and to the late Joseph Redmond for his early encouragement; to Rabbi Mark Hurvitz for advice on Jewish naming traditions and Hebrew names; to Emily Shapiro for help with Creative Class; to Rita DiMatteo for insights into Italian-American naming traditions and information on Italian names; to Richard Redmond for his keen style sense; and to the various representatives of State Departments of Health who were particularly helpful in compiling statistics on most popular names: Joseph T. Aldorisio, Greg Barber, Sue Bedard-Johnson, Charles M. Chan, Bertha Farley, Kathy Humphrys, Brian King, Verna Leilani Kong, Fred Krantz, Olga Larson, Jean LoRosso, Gary J. Sammel, Timothy Smith, Roger P. Withington, and Terri Wooten. Finally, thanks to our husbands, Christopher Finch and Richard Satran, for understanding the obsession.

INTRODUCTION

Parents used to name their babies without the help of *Beyond Jennifer & Jason*. We named our own first children that way, and it wasn't easy. Sure, there were name books, but all they told you was that Cameron meant "crooked nose" in Scotch Gaelic and Rachel was Hebrew for "female sheep." What about the real-life meanings of names? Did Cameron sound classy or pretentious, creative or wimpy? Was Rachel a classic coming back into fashion or was it already so far *in* fashion it was on its way out? We needed a guidebook that would answer these kinds of sticky questions and steer us beyond the obvious choices—the ubiquitous Jennifers and Jasons, the timeworn Johns and Marys—to names that had the brand of style, grace, distinction, intelligence, and character we wished to confer on our children.

And so we wrote one. Our aim in the original *Beyond Jennifer & Jason* was to help parents figure out how names fit into the real world their children would be entering. It seemed to us that parents deciding on something as meaningful and as permanent as a name should know, for instance, that a child named Jessica would surely be one of many and also how she would feel about that. We felt parents should have a yardstick for measuring the effects of an unusual name, an ambisexual name, a serious name on their kids, as well as an easy way to figure out which names were which.

It's no wonder, then, that *Beyond Jennifer & Jason* was born in 1988 as a full-grown hit. It was the only book available that offered parents real help in making a wise naming decision. It still is. The standard naming dictionaries may have been dusted off and given hipper covers and larger print, they may be padded with every one of the ninety-six ways to spell Alicia, but all they still tell you is that (surprise!) Cameron means "crooked nose" in Scotch Gaelic and Rachel is Hebrew for female sheep.

Meanwhile, as the first generation of children whose names were inspired by *Beyond Jennifer & Jason* fill the classrooms and the playgrounds, the world of baby-naming has grown more sophisticated, more imaginative, and more complex. The hundreds of thousands of parents inspired by the two previous editions of this book have set new standards for style in children's names, opened up new territories for exploration, deepened the general awareness of how names impact kids' futures. We've moved so far beyond Jennifer and Jason that today's parents face a greater challenge than ever in finding the right names for their babies.

That's why we're back. This new edition of *Beyond Jennifer & Jason* keeps the same format that made the original so popular, with four main sections—Style, Image, Sex, and Tradition—embracing over a hundred different lists of names organized by category: classic names and stylish names and

Irish names and African names, names to suit every taste and requirement.

But within the familiar structure you'll find lots of essential new material, including:

- A completely new Style section, with up-to-the-minute information on which names are hot and which have become overheated. Plus, hundreds of new selections for parents in search of a name on the cutting edge of style. Also, we've deepened and broadened the information in the Style section to satisfy the new wave of post-*J&J* parents who want not only the whats but the whys of a name's fashion status.
- A vastly expanded Tradition section, in tune with parents' revived interest in names that reflect their ethnic or cultural heritages. Here you'll find hundreds of new name imports from Europe and Africa, from the Jewish and Muslim traditions, from saints' names to historical favorites.
- The most complete and current news on which names are most popular according to official tallies, and on what celebrities—who have widespread influence on naming trends—are calling their babies. Also, revamped information on which famous names—real as well as fictional—are influencing what we name our children.

As before, we support our lists of names with the kind of information parents really want and need: which ambisexual names are becoming too girlish for boys, for instance, and what you should know about nicknames, middle names, and sibling names. What it's like for a boy to be a junior, and how to arrive at a name you and your spouse will both love. We've also kept to our rule of using only the most classic spellings of names. When a name has more than one accepted spelling—Catherine/Katherine, for example—we note all those that are proper, and tell you why you should think twice, make that ten times, before inventing a version of your own.

It's been gratifying, over the years since the original *Beyond Jennifer & Jason* was published, to hear from parents who tell us our book inspired them to choose names for their children they never would have arrived at on their own, names like Gray and Violet and Josephine and Miles, which they're far happier with than the more ordinary Jakes or Ashleys they might have settled for without us.

And we're gratified, too, by the parents who tell us how much they love our book, how much it helped them make the right choice of a name, how good they feel about the name as their child gets older, even when the name they pick is Jennifer or Jason.

What we want, after all, is not only to help you find the perfect name for your child, but to give you the pleasure of knowing you have made a thoughtful and enlightened choice, whether you decide to move beyond Jennifer and Jason or not.

STYLE

▼

What do we mean by style in terms of naming your baby?

Ideally, we're talking about personal style: finding a name that reflects your taste, that moves beyond fad and fashion, yet succeeds in catching the sound and spirit of the age.

Your attitudes towards style in other aspects of your life—from clothing and furniture to the way you live and your vision of the world—will affect your judgments about style in names. Whether you're conservative or liberal, care about being in fashion or rebel against it, set trends or avoid them, will all influence the style of the name you choose.

Because style changes constantly, differentiating among the names that are trendy and those that are fashionable, the names that are due for a comeback and those that are hopelessly out of date, can be difficult. That's where this section can act as your guide.

First, we outline current style: the names being used by fashionable people right now. Many of these names may not be widely popular this year, but they're heading there.

Next, you'll find a comprehensive list of the names that have been topping popularity lists for the past few years. These are the trendy names, threatened by overexposure, that you may find so far in they're out. If some of your favorites appear on this list, take heart: We also offer a selection of fresher-sounding substitutes for Jennifer, Jason, and friends.

If your desire is to find a name in the vanguard of style, the lists for you are those in the chapter of names that are so far out they're in. These are the names we believe will set the fashions for the next decade and beyond.

You may want to compare the names you like with those the rest of the world is choosing. Here you'll find lists of the most popular names in the United States, as well as a comprehensive catalog of what the rich and famous have been naming their children. The celebrity section also includes names linked to real people and fictional characters—names as accessible as Ally, as off-limits as Oprah—and why you should think twice about letting a star's popularity be your naming guide.

WHAT'S HOT

Parents today are looking for names that are both special and have real significance, not always an easy double bill to fill. The hottest names are coming from sources that had previously been left unexplored: from family trees and family Bibles, from people we admire and places we love. Gone are the names chosen from eighties-style pretensions to a glossy Ralph Lauren life; in their place are names that carry family meaning, espouse political values, signify qualities we want our children to share.

In the quest for names that meet the often-warring requirements for meaningful tradition and personal identity, parents are reviving classics that have been in mothballs for a few generations as well as fashioning first names from what had previously been surnames or place names. The newly aired classics that we call the Volvo names—names like Jack and Henry and Isabel—as well as the Biblical boys' names are the hottest in terms of popularity: they're favored by the largest number and widest variety of parents. The family names and place names that are now being translated into first names— Cameron and Avery, Catalina and Austin—are the hottest in terms of style.

But names from all those classifications, like hot names of the past, are forever in danger of flaring into trendiness, of burning so brightly they lose the spark that made them hot in the first place. Choosing a name that's hot is always risky: You may select one that remains brilliant without burning out, or you may find your choice overheating once it's too late to drop it.

The wisest course, then, is to arm yourself with knowledge about which names are hot, and why, before you make your selection. Here are the hot names right now.

THE VOLVO NAMES

The hottest names today are what we call the Volvo names: solid, dependable, trend-resistant, classy but not flashy, chic of the reverse kind. They're the names of kings and queens, heiresses and presidents, as well as many of our own more ordinary ancestors—which accounts for a good measure of their popularity. Many parents today are turning their backs on fashion and looking to their own families as the source of names for their babies.

While the conservative tone of the eighties did much to restore traditional names to favor, now we're not conserva-tive so much as family-oriented, turning towards our own homes and histories for meaning and sustenance. Why, many parents feel, choose a name for mere melody or style when you can select one that carries real resonance over generations? Trendy choices like Leaf or Lisa or Lindsay seem disposable compared with naming your child after Great-grandma Laura.

tions? Trendy choices like Leaf or Lisa or Lindsay seem disposable compared with naming your child after Great-grandma Laura.

And, in this age of recycling, we're against disposability. We want things that last. That's why even parents who don't have a Margaret or a Henry or a Helen or a Paul in their family trees are choosing these sorts of time-honored names for their children.

The one major problem with the Volvo names is: Which ones will retain their immutably classic, beyond-fashion feel and which are in danger of tipping over the edge into trendiness? While a name like Elizabeth has survived too long to ever descend to the here-today, gone-tomorrow faddishness of, say, Kayla, it has become the tenth most popular girls' name, and your own little Elizabeth or Lizzie is destined forever to be one of several in her peer group.

Of course, if you're choosing one of these names to honor someone significant within your family, you may not be overly concerned with its fashion status. But if you want to avoid the traditional names that, like Elizabeth, have become overused, see Fashionable Classics, page 24. And if you want to be certain to move in the other direction and choose a name not yet in general favor, consult Can You Really Name a Baby Edna?, page 31. The fact is, although an Elizabeth will always weather more miles than a Kayla, there are no long-term warranties on any of the Volvo names: because of their very familiarity and potentially wide appeal, any of them could slip from hot to overheated.

The Volvo names

G I R L S

ALICE
CAROLINE
CHARLOTTE
CLAIRE
ELEANOR
ELIZA
EVE
FAITH
FRANCES
GRACE
HELEN
HOPE
ISABEL ✓
JANE
JOANNA
JULIA

LOUISE
LUCY
MADEL(E)INE
MARGARET
MARTHA
MIRANDA
NATALIE
NELL
NORA
OLIVIA
ROSE
SALLY
SOPHIA
SUSANNAH
TESS
VIRGINIA

B O Y S

CHARLES
EDWARD
FREDERICK
GEORGE
HENRY
HUGH
JACK
JOHN

JOSEPH
PATRICK
PAUL
PETER
PHIL(L)IP
ROBERT
THOMAS

The Max and Sam of the Nineties?

We like the names Jack and Henry. So do a lot of other people. It seems as if every expectant parent we know has narrowed the field of boys' names to Jack or Henry, following the lead of Susan Sarandon and Tim Robbins, Meg Ryan and Dennis Quaid, Ellen Barkin and Gabriel Byrne, Julia Louis-Dreyfuss and Brad Hall, Corbin Bernsen and Amanda Pays, Dennis Hopper, Willem Dafoe, and Ozzie Osbourne—all of whom have a new little Jack or Henry of their own. When we met a mother in the playground the other day whose preschoolers were named the ultra-trendy Caitlin and Zack, and whose baby was named Henry ("but my husband wanted to call him Jack"), the fate of those two names was all but sealed. Jack and Henry seem destined to become the Max and Sam of the nineties.

Do Jack and Henry have a female equivalent, similarly in jeopardy of rampant overuse? If we had to choose one, it would be, sigh, another favorite: Isabel.

A Rose After Any Other Name

For the first time since the 1950s, when nearly every girl was given the middle name of Ann or Marie or Lynn, there is a middle name that seems to be favored by an amazingly large group of parents: Rose. This defies the fashion of the past three decades, which mandated no middle name or one with family significance, especially mother's maiden name or the names of grandparents. But Rose has gone wild as a middle name whether it's attached to a family member or not. It's used to soften androgynous first names so popular for girls today, it's given because many parents like it but not enough to choose it for a first name, and it's also popular because, like Ann and Marie, it simply provides a smooth bridge between a child's first and last names.

HEROES AND HEROINES

All of a sudden we started hearing it everywhere: the name Miles. Where did this come from? we wondered. Miles didn't fit into any fashionable categories; it was not a name that had been the kind of whisper we might expect to swell to a roar. And, then, one of the celebrities who'd named his child Miles (was it Tim Robbins or Eddie Murphy?) was quoted as saying he was honoring a personal hero, jazz musician Miles Davis.

This we can understand. In fact, along with naming babies after notable people in one's family, choosing names of heroes and heroines from the worlds of music, art, literature, sports, and politics has become a hot trend. Rod Steiger, for instance (yes, the sixty-something-year-old Rod Steiger), says his new son, Michael Winston, is named after two heroes, Michelangelo and Winston Churchill. And we strongly suspect that John Travolta's choice of Jett paid homage to James Dean's Jett Rink character in *Giant* and that Sean Penn's Hopper Jack had something to do with Dennis.

Like family names, the Hero and Heroine names have meaning and history; they honor people we'd like our children to emulate, symbolize traits we hope our children will share. The hottest among them also catch the flavor of the times; however admirable the people, for instance, we haven't heard of parents naming their babies after Sigmund Freud or Yehudi Menuhin. The following, though, are hot and getting hotter:

Heroes and heroines

F E M A L E

AMELIA Earhart
ANAÏS Nin
AUDREY Hepburn
BEATRIX Potter
CHARLOTTE Brontë
COCO Chanel

COLETTE
EDITH Wharton
ELEANOR Roosevelt
ELLA Fitzgerald
EMMA Goldman/
    Bovary/Jane Austen's

FLANNERY O'Connor
FRIDA Kahlo
GEORGIA O'Keeffe
GRACE Kelly
HARRIET Beecher
  Stowe/Tubman
HILLARY Rodham
  Clinton
ISADORA Duncan
JANE Austen/Eyre
JOSEPHINE Baker

LOUISA May Alcott
NORA (*A Doll's House*)
  Helmer
ROXANE, beloved of
  Cyrano
SCARLETT O'Hara
SIMONE de Beauvoir
TESS (of the
  D'Urbervilles)
WILLA Cather
ZELDA Fitzgerald

M A L E

ADLAI Stevenson
AMADEUS Mozart,
  Wolfgang
BO Jackson
BYRON (Lord)
COLIN Powell
DASHIELL Hammett
DYLAN Thomas/Bob
  DYLAN
ELVIS Presley
FRANK Lloyd Wright
HENRY/HANK Aaron
HOLDEN Caulfield
JESSE Jackson
JONAS Salk
KAREEM Abdul Jabar

LIONEL Hampton/
  Trilling
LOUIS Armstrong
MALCOLM X
MICHAEL Jordan
MILES Davis
OTIS Redding
PATRICK Ewing
RALPH WALDO
  Emerson
RAY Charles
WALKER Percy
WILL Rogers
WILLIE Mays
WINSTON Churchill
ZANE Grey

PRESIDENTIAL NAMES

A special category must be set aside for Presidential names—not names that sound as if they might get your child elected to our country's highest office one day, as may have been the trend in the eighties, but the names, first and last, of actual U.S. Presidents. The surname-names among them are being considered for girls as well as boys. Here, a sampling of those we've been hearing:

Presidential names

ABRAHAM	JEFFERSON
CARTER	KENNEDY
CLINTON	LINCOLN
FRANKLIN	MADISON
GEORGE	MONROE
GRANT	TRUMAN
HARRISON	ULYSSES
HARRY	WILSON
JACK	WOODROW
JACKSON	

FAMILY NAMES

Waspy surname-names—Jordan and Morgan, Lindsay and Whitney—emerged in the eighties to become wildly popular, initially for boys but, as the decade marched on, increasingly for girls. As a group, they perfectly captured the spirit of the decade, combining a feminist viewpoint with executive power and an old-money feel. These names became so widely used, in fact, that several—Courtney, Kelsey, Shelby, Tyler, Jordan, Taylor, Brooke, Page, Evan—have jumped from obscurity to the most-popular lists in a mere decade, with Ashley rocketing to number one for girls.

While this trend continues to be hot, many parents have progressed from choosing names based on a Ralph Lauren-style simulation of tradition to those that have a genuine connection to their families. A mother's maiden name, a maternal grandfather's surname, any last name with real family roots may be preferable to one that's pulled out of the air. After much televised debate, for instance, Murphy Brown gave her baby boy her mother's name, Avery.

Those parents with ethnic names may devise some variation: DiMatteo can become Matteo, O'Connell can be shortened to simply Connell. The bold may want to use an ethnic family name unabridged: If you can name a baby Cooper, why not Perez or Chan or Weber? Other parents, finding no suitable surnames in their own families, may still be attracted to this group for their sons or daughters and may want to look to this list for inspiration. Among the hottest family names on the scene now:

Family names

ADDISON	BROWN
AMORY	CAMERON
AVERY	CAMPBELL
BAILEY	CARSON
BRODY	CARTER

CASSIDY	MASON
CLAY	MURPHY
COLE	NICHOLSON
COOPER	PARKER
DALTON	PEYTON
DAWSON	PORTER
EVERETT	QUINN
FINN	REED
FLANNERY	RILEY
FLYNN	SAWYER
FORREST	SHAW
FOSTER	SHEA
GRAY	SLOAN
HARPER	SMITH
HART	TAYLOR
HUNTER	TUCKER
KENNEDY	WADE
KENYON	WALKER
LANE	WILEY
LOGAN	WYATT
MACKENZIE	

Why Cameron and Taylor Will Never Be Hot Names in Norway

According to Norwegian Name Law, Paragraph 15, Number 2 (no, we're not kidding), parents are forbidden from giving their children names "that are or have been used as surnames and are not originally first names." Among those names prohibited: Russell, as in Bertrand, and Scott, as in Sir Walter.

Surname-names are permitted for use as middle names, provided they carry some genuine family connection. The mother's maiden name is okay; so is the earlier surname of an adopted child. But if parents want to give their child a surname-middle name with less evident family ties, they have to prove to the government that the name has "special affiliation through the family or some other way." Just thinking it's cute, in other words, is not reason enough.

The Norwegian Name Law also forbids any name that is "a disadvantage to whom it is given." Examples cited: Adolph and Elvis. New on the law's forbidden list: animal names, which means there will be no more Bjorns (translation: bear) in Norway.

PLACE NAMES

The most explosive group of hot names, place names, have gone from the relative obscurity of the So Far Out They're In lists in our last two editions to the forefront of fashion. Celebrities who sport place names—notably Winona Ryder, Dakota Jackson, Chelsea Clinton, and Cuba Gooding, Jr.— have helped bring the concept to a wide audience. And the stars who've rushed to choose their babies' names from maps have further popularized the practice: Melanie Griffith and

Don Johnson as well as Melissa Gilbert both have little Dakotas, Nastassja Kinski and Quincy Jones have an infant
Kenya, Sissy Spacek has a Madison, David Carradine a girl
named Kansas, director Jonathan Demme's new child is
named Brooklyn, Montana is the middle name of Woody
Harrelson's baby daughter, guru Marianne Williamson and
Catherine Oxenburg have Indias, and Mick Jagger and Jerry
Hall named their newest daughter Georgia, after the state
where she was conceived. Mick's first grandchild also has a
place name—she's a girl called Assisi.

As Mick and Jerry did, choosing a place name with personal significance is the hottest of this hot trend: You can
name your child after the place your grandparents were born,
where you honeymooned, or where your child was conceived,
be it a small town in Pennsylvania or an island off the coast
of Turkey. You don't have to restrict your inspired map-
reading to towns and cities, either: rivers, oceans, mountains,
and even mythical places are all fair game.

With the range of place names as wide as the world, some
choices will obviously be unique, others will remain unusual,
but the most accessible and widely used will continue to
heat up to the boiling point. The white-hot place names
today are:

Place names

G I R L S

AFRICA	CHELSEA
ASIA	CHINA
CAROLINA	EDEN

GENEVA	KENYA
GEORGIA	SAVANNAH
INDIA	WINONA

A M B I S E X U A L

BOSTON	MADISON
DAKOTA	MONTANA
DEVON	PORTLAND
JERSEY	SIERRA

B O Y S

AUSTIN	MACON
DALLAS	TROY
JACKSON	

Other choices we've heard, primarily for girls but a few suitable for boys as well, include:

ALABAMA	FLORENCE
AMERICA	FLORIDA
ATLANTA	FRANCE
BRAZIL	HOLLAND
BROOKLYN	HOUSTON
CATALINA	INDIANA
CAIRO	ISRAEL
CHEYENNE	ITHACA
CUBA	JAMAICA
DENVER	LONDON
EGYPT	LOUISIANA
ELBA	MAYO

MEMPHIS	SIENA
MIAMI	TENNESSEE
NEVADA	TRIPOLI
ODESSA	TULSA
PARIS	VENETIA
PERSIA	VENICE
PHOENIX	VERONA
RIO	VIENNA
ROMA	ZAIRE

"Imagine your name is Dakota and you go to play school and there are five others," says Wendy, who met two Dakotas last week. "Couples are actually going through the states, Carolina, Indiana, Florida. What's next? New York? There's already a kid named Jersey on my block."

—Margot Kaufman, *Los Angeles Times Magazine*

BIBLICAL BOYS

With many of the hottest groups of names suitable for both boys and girls, it's unusual to hit upon a category that seems to be hot for boys alone. But the hot Biblical names are all masculine ones partly because the Bible itself contains many more male names than female ones. As Biblical names have been in general favor over the past few decades, many of the feminine choices—Rebecca, Rachel, Sarah, Hannah—have skipped up to the most-popular lists along with their most widely used male counterparts—Joshua, Matthew, Jacob, Zachary, Jonathan, and Aaron.

The large group of parents who favor Biblical names, whether because of religious interest or a taste for things traditional, are now often looking for fresher choices. Many of the selections that remain are still unusual enough to be relegated to the So Far Out They're In section (see page 21); others, primarily the boys' names listed here, have become newly fashionable:

Biblical boys

CALEB

ELI

ELIJAH

GABRIEL

GIDEON

JARED

JEREMIAH

JONAH

NATHANIEL

NOAH

SIMON

TOBIAS

ZACHARIAH

So Far in They're Out

The whole issue of trendiness in names is a double-edged sword. For the most part, kids like having popular names; they like swimming in the mainstream. You wouldn't find many seven-year-old Samanthas, Seans, or Sams out there who would say they hated their names. (Unless, perhaps, if there were three other Samanthas in their class.) On the other hand, there might be quite a few twenty-seven-year-old Sharis, Scotts, or Shelleys who would voice some regrets at being known to the world by those epidemic names of the sixties.

We present the following master list of So Far In They're Out Names so that if you choose one of them for your child, it will be with the knowledge that these names carry with them the dilemma of trendiness. Even if there aren't any Brandons or Caitlins or Jordans on your block yet, it doesn't mean they aren't trendy names. As fresh as some of them may sound to your ear, there's a good chance that a couple of other kids with the same name will be in your child's kindergarten class.

But what if Nicole is your favorite name despite its trendy status? Either forge ahead with it, knowing that your Nicole will bring something unique to the name, or consult the substitution guide that follows.

So far in they're out names

G I R L S

ALEXANDRA
ALEXIS
ALLISON
ALYSSA
AMANDA √
AMBER
AMY
ANNIE
ARIEL
ASHLEY
BRIANNA
BRITTANY/
    BRITTNEY
BROOKE
CAITLIN
CHELSEA
CHRISTIE
COURTNEY
CRYSTAL
DANIELLE
DAWN
ERICA

HALEY √
HEATHER
JENNA
JENNIFER
JENNY
JESSICA
JESSIE
JORDAN
KAYLA √
KELLY
KELSEY
KIMBERLY
KIRSTEN
KRISTEN
LAUREN
LINDSEY
LIZZIE
MAGGIE
MEGAN
MELANIE
MELISSA
MICHELLE

MOLLY
MORGAN
NICOLE
SAMANTHA
SHELBY

STEPHANIE
TAYLOR
TIFFANY
VANESSA
WHITNEY

B O Y S

AARON
ADAM
ALEX
ALEXANDER
ASHLEY
AUSTIN
BEN
BENJAMIN
BRADLEY
BRANDON
BRENDAN
BRIAN
CAMERON
CASEY
CODY
COREY
DEREK
DUSTIN
DYLAN
ERIC
ETHAN
GREGORY
IAN
JACOB

JAKE
JARED
JASON
JEREMY
JESSE
JONATHAN
JORDAN
JOSHUA
JUSTIN
KEVIN
KYLE
MAX
NATHAN
RYAN
SAM
SAMUEL
SEAN
TAYLOR
TRAVIS
TREVOR
TYLER ✓
ZACHARY
ZACK

FASHIONABLE CLASSICS

Fashionable classics are names that, while they happen to be trendy right now, nonetheless have staying power. If you give your child one of these fashionable classic names, you should know that he or she will be one of many with the same name. Nevertheless, these names won't necessarily brand him forever as a child of the nineties, the way their faddier cousins—Joshua, Jessica, et al.—might.

Some of the following are among the most widely used names on the Restored Classics list; others figure prominently on most-popular lists around the country. What we consider fashionable classics are:

G I R L S

ANNA√	KATE
CHRISTINA	KATHERINE
CHRISTINE	LAURA
ELIZABETH	RACHEL
EMILY	REBECCA
EMMA	SARAH

B O Y S

ANDREW	MATTHEW
CHRISTOPHER	MICHAEL
DANIEL	NICHOLAS
DAVID	TIMOTHY
JAMES	WILLIAM

My friend Wendy is aunt to Ruby, Tripoli, Matisse, and Jake. "Cathy and Barbara are beginning to sound good to me," Wendy says. "I'm so sick of some of these yuppie names I can hardly get them out of my mouth. Like Zoe, Chelsea and Dakota."

—Margot Kaufman, *Los Angeles Times Magazine*

BUT NICOLE IS MY FAVORITE NAME!

If all the foregoing has depressed you, if you've wanted to name your daughter Nicole since you were twelve years old and were not aware that thousands of other people had the same idea, we offer in apology a selection of names you might consider substituting for too-trendy favorites. What you consider an overused name or an acceptable substitute is to some extent a matter of personal style. Not all of the names on the "instead of" list have been pegged as so far in they're out, and some of the substitutes make a big leap forward in fashion. However, all of the possible substitute names bear some relationship to their overexposed counterparts in sound, feel, or taste, but their color is brighter and their texture a bit crisper.

G I R L S

Instead of:	Consider:
ALEXANDRA	ARABELLA
ALLISON	ALICE ✓
ALYSSA	ELIZA
AMANDA	MIRANDA ✓
AMBER	RUBY
ASHLEY	AVERY ✓
CAITLIN	BRONWEN
COURTNEY	SYDNEY
DANA	DINAH
DANIELLE	LUCIENNE or DIANTHA
EMILY	EMILIA or EMELINE
ERIN	DEVON or ESMÉ
HALEY	HAZEL
JENNIFER	GENEVIEVE
JESSICA	JESSA or JESSAMINE
JESSIE	JOSIE
JORDAN	GEORGIA
KELLY	QUINN
KIMBERLY	KIRBY
KRISTIN	INGRID or VIVEKA
LAUREN	LAUREL
LINDSAY	LACEY ✓
LISA	LOUISA
MEGAN	REGAN or MARGARET
MELISSA	PRISCILLA or LARISSA
MOLLY	POLLY or DAISY

NICOLE	NICOLA
RACHEL	TAMAR
SAMANTHA	SUSANNAH
SHANNON	SHEA
TARA	NORA
TIFFANY	TESSA
TRACY	GRACE/GRACIE ✓
VANESSA·	VIOLET or
	CASSANDRA

B O Y S

Instead of:	Consider:
AARON	ABNER or ABEL
ADAM	ASA
ALEX	ALEC or AXEL
BRANDON	BRAM
BRIAN	BRENNAN or BYRON
CAMERON	CLEMENT
CASEY	CLANCY or CASPER
CHRISTOPHER	CHRISTIAN
CODY	BRODY
DYLAN	DEXTER
ERIC	EMMETT
JACOB	CALEB
JAKE	ABE
JASON	JASPER
JEREMY	JEREMIAH or JARVIS
JONATHAN	JONAS or JOHN
JORDAN	GEORGE
JOSHUA	JOSIAH
JUSTIN	JULIAN

KEVIN	CALVIN
LUKE	LEVI
MATTHEW	MATTHIAS
MAX	HARRY
NICHOLAS	THADDEUS
RYAN	RILEY ✓
SAM	GUS or SIMM
SAMUEL	SAMSON or LEMUEL
SEAN	SHAW or FERGUS
ZACHARY	ZACHARIAH
ZACK	ZEKE

Since it seems to me that this fad of child-rearing has turned into an actual trend, that babies are an increasingly popular accessory for people-on-the-go, I first want to say to stop naming your boys Max. Max is a perfectly nice name, ensuring in its owner a certain precocious sensibility, but there are enough Maxes now. Any more Maxes and the breed will go to the dogs.

—Cynthia Heimel, *If You Can't Live Without Me, Why Aren't You Dead Yet?*

In a Political Correctness quiz, *Los Angeles Magazine* posed the following question:
#5. What name did you give your first child?

(A) I expect my child to discover his or her
own name and totem.
(B) Molly, Zoe or Cody
(C) Max, Oliver or Cody
(D) I *think* she calls him Ed.

The other day at a restaurant . . . Hannah was
admiring a baby who was swathed in pink in
her father's arms. Hannah really wanted to take
this baby home. . . . The baby's father seemed
charmed.

"What's her name?" he asked me.

"Hannah," said I.

"Hers too," the man said, thrilled, like we
were members of the same club. I was
considerably less sanguine.

Turns out there's a little girl named Hannah who
lives across the street from this baby Hannah at the
restaurant. And it turns out that my former editor
now has a Hannah, and there's another Hannah
who belongs to a friend at work.

When this friend and I talk about our
offspring, we start off by distinguishing between
my Hannah and *yours*.

To all you other young Hannahs out there: I
don't want to know.

—Dianne Klein, *Los Angeles Times*

So FAR OUT THEY'RE IN

As names like Hannah and Henry, Derek and Dakota climb the style ladder from hip to decidedly overheated, which new groups of names do we see emerging to take their place?

We predict that the predominant naming trend of the past few years—the search for names with family, ethnic, or personal significance—will explode over the next decade, as parents explore brand-new territory for names that both carry some weight and set their children apart from the crowd. The style boundaries that had been drawn around traditional names revived for the last decade's babies will be expanded to include scores of old-time choices long deemed too musty for modern kids. With the increasing emphasis on home and comfort and family, we'll seek to recycle familiar names in fresh ways. And as the world shrinks, many parents will import names from other countries—either the countries where their grandparents were born, or places where they've traveled.

What we'll be hearing, over the next several years, are

scores of old names played for the first time in generations, and others making their debut on our shores. The hundreds of choices that follow here all have style but aren't trendy, sound fresh but not invented, are solid but never boring.

On Becoming a Walter

You can't be Walter in a pram. You can't be Walter until you're about seventy-five in my view. So if they're going to christen you Walter they'd better put a couple of names in front of it, one for your spell in the pram plus another for the long haul up to becoming Walter . . . they might call you Robin Bartholomew Walter, for example.

—Julian Barnes, *Talking It Over*

CAN YOU REALLY NAME A BABY EDNA?

Until now, the fashion for naming babies after family members has focused on choosing a name that was both substantial and stylish, with the emphasis on style. Parents have pored over family trees in search of names that sounded congenial to the modern ear, however obscure or colorless the ancestors they honored. But the resulting abundance of little Katherines and Elizabeths, Williams and Sams has prompted some parents to approach their quest from the opposite direction, to choose the honoree first and trust that he or she will confer individual chic on what otherwise might be thought of as a dowdy name. Why not—some parents are starting to ask—name the baby Leopold, after the great-grandfather who rode in the cavalry in the Civil War and became a state senator? Taken in that context, the name Leopold acquires dash and style as well as history.

The nagging question: Can you really name a baby Leopold, or Willard, or Edna? Of course you can. The new generation of parents brave enough to revive their own long-dormant ancestor names has pumped fresh life into this entire group. Suddenly, these names that have moldered in the attic for so long seem stylish again. Granted, many of them will remain more prevalent on gravestones and in old-age homes than in playgrounds a bit longer—but that's part of the point, isn't it? If you're attracted to this kind of name, you're after something that will stand apart from the crowd of cute baby names.

The only remaining question: Where do you draw the line? If Edna has the capacity for chic, can Ethel be far behind? Is any name—Seymour or Murray or Bertha or Thelma—so musty it deserves to be thrown away once and for all? Well, that's hard to say. In one sense, the only valid place to mark a boundary is at the names that are important within one's own family. But even with family matters aside, this group of names has made such rapid and surprising progress from outmoded to chic that we hesitate to relegate any individual choices—no matter how terminally dated they may seem—to the wastebasket. For now, however, we see the following as most ready for revival:

Edna names

G I R L S

ADA	ESTHER
ADELAIDE	EUDORA
ADELIA	EUGENIA
ADELINE	EUNICE
AGATHA	EVA
AGNES	EVANGELINE
ALMA	EVELYN
AMELIA	FAITH
ANASTASIA	FAY
ANTONIA	FLORA
AUGUSTA	FLORENCE
AVIS	FRANCES
BELVA	FREDERICA
BERNADETTE	GENEVIEVE
BLANCHE	GERALDINE
CLARA	GWENDOLYN
CONSTANCE	HARRIET
CORA	HAZEL
CORDELIA	HELENA
CORNELIA	HENRIETTA
DOROTHEA	IDA
EDNA	IMOGEN(E)
EDWINA	IOLA
ELLA	IONE
ELSA	IVY
ELVIRA	JOSEPHINE
ENID	KAY
ESMÉ	LEONORA

LETITIA
LOUELLA
LOUISA
MARIAN
MARIE
MATILDA
MAUD(E)
MAVIS
MAY
MERLE
MILLICENT
MINERVA
MURIEL
OLIVE

PAULINE
PEARL
PENELOPE
PRISCILLA
PRUDENCE
ROSALIND
SYBIL
SYLVIA
THEODORA
URSULA
VIOLET
WILHELMINA
WINIFRED
ZELDA

B O Y S

ALBERT
ALFRED
AMBROSE
ARCHIBALD
ARCHIE
AUGUST
AUGUSTINE
AUGUSTUS
BARTHOLOMEW
BORIS
CALVIN
CASPER
CHESTER
CLIFFORD
CLYDE

CONRAD
CORNELIUS
CYRUS
DEXTER
EDGAR
EDMUND
ELIAS
EMMETT
FELIX
FERGUS
FLOYD
FRANCIS
FRANKLIN
GILBERT
GODFREY

GORDON	MARTIN
HAROLD	MORTIMER
HECTOR	PERCY
HIRAM	QUINCY
HORACE	RAYMOND
HUGO	RICHARD
HUMPHREY	ROLAND
IGNATIUS	THEODORE
ISIDORE	VICTOR
JASPER	VIRGIL
LEO	WALTER
LEOPOLD	WILLARD
LIONEL	WINSTON
LLOYD	WOLFGANG
LOUIS/LEWIS	WOODROW

HOMESTYLE

Everyone's staying at home these days, nobody has any money, and down-to-earth names that reject gloss in favor of comfort seem hipper than ever. In fact, another tagline for this group could be the Comfort Names: familiar as an old T-shirt, soft as Grandma's easy chair, warm as a hand-knit afghan, they don't aim to impress or intimidate or brazen their way through the world. Even the most unusual among them seem friendly and relaxed.

The Homestyle Names easing in to replace worn-out counterparts like Sam and Max, Annie and Maggie, include these:

Homestyle names

G I R L S

ABBIE/ABBY
BELLE
BESS
CEIL
CHARITY
CLOVER
COMFORT
DAISY
DALE
DELLA
DORA
DULCY
FANNY
HATTIE
JOSIE
KITTY
LIBBY
LULU
MABEL

MAE
MAGNOLIA
MAISIE
MAMIE
MERCY
MILLIE
MITZI
PATIENCE
PATSY
POLLY
ROXY
RUBY
SADIE
SONIA
SOPHIE
STELLA
WILLA
WINNIE

B O Y S

ABE
ABNER
CAL
CLEM
CY
FRANK

FRED
GUS
HAL
HANK
HARRY
HARVEY

HOMER	OTIS
IKE	RALPH
JETHRO	RAY
MOE	SILAS
NAT	TY
NED	ZEKE
OSCAR	

THE LESSER BIBLICALS

Biblical names have been in favor for an entire generation of children now, with the most popular—Sarah and Joshua and Benjamin and Rachel—climbing to the top of the charts, and others—notably Hannah and Jacob and Nathan and Sam—hot on their heels. But today's parents, whether motivated by religion or tradition, are not about to abandon Biblical names as a group just because they've become trendy; they're simply delving into the Bible for fresher choices. Some of these—Biblical boys' names such as Nathaniel and Noah and Caleb—have quickly become so popular they're now in our What's Hot section; others, such as the names that follow, are still on the cutting edge of fashion.

Biblical names

G I R L S

ABIGAIL	DEBORAH/
ADINA	DEVORAH
BETHIA	DELILAH

DINAH
ESTHER
EVE
JEMIMA
JUDITH
KETURAH
KEZIAH
LYDIA

MARA
MICHAL
MIRIAM
NAOMI
RUTH
SARAI
TAMAR

B O Y S

ABEL
ABNER
ABRAHAM
ADLAI
AMOS
ASA
ASHER
DARIUS
EMANUEL
ENOCH
EPHRAIM
ESAU
EZEKIEL
EZRA
HIRAM
ISAAC
ISAIAH

JOAH
JOSIAH
JUDAH
LEVI
MALACHI
MICAH
MOSES
OMAR
PHINEAS
RAPHAEL
REUBEN
SAMSON
SAUL
SIMEON
SOLOMON
ZEBEDIAH

Lettuce Alone

Just when we thought we were running out of excruciatingly original girls' names (Moon Unit and China being hopelessly passé), along came best-selling author Banana Yoshimoto, trailing a garden of possibilities. The new nineties monikers: Arugula, Clove, and of course, Valencia. . . .

—*Mirabella* magazine

A GIRL NAMED THOMAS

It started in the sixties, with girls getting their share of the new crop of cute ambisexual names: Jody and Kelly, Jamie and Kerry. It exploded in the eighties as a new generation of feminist working mothers gave their daughters equal access to fashionable androgynous names, surname-names and place names: Jordan and Morgan, Taylor and Dakota. Now, girls' names are breaking through the final frontier, invading naming territory that has long been a male bastion.

Celebrities with men's names—Glenn Close, Daryl Hannah, Sean Young, Drew Barrymore—have helped forge the path into this new area. A few stars have selected boys' names for their daughters: Sting has a little girl named Eliot, and Andy Garcia has a female Dominik. There was a prime-time television female lead character named Wally; the heroine of P. D. James's best-selling *The Children of Men* was named Julian; and the female narrator of a recent *New Yorker* story was called Clay. In real life, we know women named Dean, Neil, Seth, James, and Jay, and another whose middle name is Dick.

While the innovation of giving boys' names to girls may seem to be an historical first, it was in fact common practice in Olde England, where girls were commonly called Alexander, Aubrey, Basil, Douglas, Edmund, Eustace, Gilbert, Giles, James, Nicholas, Philip, Reynold, and Simon. These days, once a name crosses the line from masculine to feminine, it's unusual for it ever to travel back again. As more and more previously all-boy names are claimed by girls, we worry that boys will have fewer decidedly masculine choices left.

Still, many boys' names acquire new life when used for girls. Somehow, all the baggage associated with the name falls away and you're suddenly able to hear its intrinsic rhythm and sound. Names that have become outdated for boys—Vincent or Stanley or Leonard—seem melodic and jaunty and stylish again. While introducing the idea theoretically opens up the entire field of masculine names to girls, we think the following sound the most apt:

A girl named Thomas

ADAM	ANDREW
ALAN	BARNABY
AMOS	BRADLEY

CHRISTOPHER	LAWRENCE/
CLAUDE	LAURENCE
CLAY	LEONARD
CLIFFORD	LLOYD
DARRIN	LUCIAN
DARYL	MICHAEL
DEAN	NEAL/NEIL
DOMINIC	NICHOLAS
DORIAN	PHILIP
DOUGLAS	QUENTIN
DUNCAN	QUINCY
DUSTIN✓	REUBEN
EL(L)IOT	RICHARD
EVAN	ROSS
GEORGE	ROY
GLENN	SCOTT
GORDON	SETH
IAN	SIDNEY
JAMES	SPENCER
JAY	STANLEY
JEREMY	THOMAS
JULIAN	TIMOTHY
JUSTIN	TYLER
KENNETH	VINCENT
KENT	ZACHARY
KEVIN	ZANE

Well, it's better than Elvisina

Rocker Jon Bon Jovi told *People* magazine he didn't know the sex of the baby he and his wife were expecting, but it didn't matter . . . at least in terms of a name. "The pending name is Elvis," Bon Jovi said, "because that could be for a boy or a girl."

EXOTICA

Names are crossing the ocean in record numbers as America joins the global village and parents look further afield in search of names that are at once distinctive and reflect family heritage. The hottest of these exotic names are those familiar in the English-speaking world: names with Latin backgrounds that are often used in England and adapted by many European cultures, British favorites that until now haven't hit our shores, and Irish and Scottish names.

Many parents will find these names appealing beyond the consideration of culture: Whatever your ethnic background, an exotic name can make for an unusual, melodic choice. The ultrafeminine girls' names in this group provide a nice counterpoint to the ambisexual and masculine names increasingly used for girls, and many of the choices for boys at once sound newer than the traditional selections such as John and Michael and stronger than trendy names like Kyle and Justin.

For those parents who specifically want names that reflect

their own heritage—and for those who want to explore even deeper into exotic territory—consult also the ethnic name lists in the Tradition section of this book.

Here, exotica destined for wide appeal:

Exotic names

G I R L S

ADRIANA
ALLEGRA
ANGELICA
ANTHEA
ARABELLA
ASTRID
AURELIA
AURORA
BIANCA
BRONWEN
CANDIDA
CARINA ✓
CARLOTTA
CARMEN ✓
CASSANDRA
CHANTAL
CHIARA
CLEO
CONSUELO
COSIMA
CRESSIDA
DARIA

DELPHINA
DIANTHA
ELENA ✓
ELODIE
ESMÉ
FLAVIA
FLEUR
FRANCESCA
GABRIELLA
GEMMA
GIOIA
INGRID
ISABELLA
JASMINE
JOCASTA
JUNO
LAYLA
LEILA
LELIA
LETHIA
LILIANA
LIV

LOLA
LUCIA
MARIA
MARIAH
MARIAN(N)A
MARIELLA
MERCEDES
MIRABEL
NATALYA
NATANIA
NATASHA
NICOLA
OCTAVIA
ODELIA
OLYMPIA
OPHELIA
ORIANA
OTTILIE
PALMA
PALOMA
PANDORA
PERDITA
PETRA
PIA
PILAR
PORTIA

QUINTINA
RAFFAELA
RAMONA
RENATA
ROMILLY
ROMY
SABRINA
SAFFRON
SELENA
SERAPHINA/
   SERAFINA
SERENA
SHOSHANA
SIMONE
TABITHA
TAMARA
TANIA
TATIANA
TAVIA
TERTIA
THALIA
VALENTINA
VENETIA
VERENA
YASMINE

B O Y S

ALDO
ALONZO
ANATOLE

ANDRÉ
ANTON
ARLO

ARNO	LUCIUS
BALTHAZAR	MATTHIAS
BARNABUS	MILO
BENNO	NICO
BORIS	OCTAVIUS
BRUNO	OMAR
COSMO	ORLANDO
DAMIAN	OTTO
ELMO	PABLO
EMILIO	PAOLO
FABIAN	PHILIPPE
GUNTHER	PHILO
HORATIO	PIERS
IVOR	RAOUL
JARVIS	RUFUS
LARS	THEO
LUCAS ✓	TITUS
LUCIEN	WALDO

In those days I had little inclination toward being a parent, yet I imagined playing with my progeny and wondered what I'd call them. Soon I came up with Praline for a girl (this came to me one night during dessert), and Conch for a boy (a visit to Marineland). Perhaps it was the common ring of my brothers' names that led them to dub their daughters Dalisa, Cambria,

and Jordana, names as strange as orchids at
the florists. . . .

—Bernard Cooper, *Maps to Anywhere*

Some of those exotic models we see smoldering
on the pages of magazines have some pretty
exotic names as well. For example, the following
were spotted in a recent IMG's model book: Ali,
Cha Cha, Chanin, Chrystelle, Elza, Erickka,
Gabrielle, Italiaia, Josefina, Keeli, La Roe, Na-
dya, Tara, Tanya, and Tonya. Other successful
models include Frauke, Shalom, Vendela, Ariane,
Kajsa, Dalma, Yasmine, and Natane.

THE BRITS

The Brits may speak the same language as we do, but they
do so with a different accent. So too are many of their names
familiar, while others retain an exotic ring. British names
poised for invasion include these:

British names

G I R L S

ARAMINTA
CAMILLA
CARO
CECILY
CICELY
CLARISSA
CLEMENCY
CLEMENTINE
DAHLIA
DAPHNE
EMELINE
FELICITY
FLORA
GEORGINA

GILLIAN
HONOR
IMOGEN
IONA
JESSAMINE
JESSAMY
MAVIS
MILLICENT
PHILIPPA
PIPPA
POPPY
POSY
ROSAMOND
UNITY

B O Y S

ADRIAN
ALEC
ALISTAIR
AMBROSE
BASIL
CLEMENT
CLIVE
COLIN
CRISPIN
CYRIL
DAMIAN

DESMOND
FELIX
GILES
GRAHAM
GUY
HUGO
INIGO
IVOR
JASPER
JULIAN
LIONEL

NEVILLE	ROLF
NIGEL	ROLLO
NOEL	RUPERT
PERCY	SEBASTIAN
QUENTIN	TREVOR
REX	TRISTAN ✓

THE SCOTS

From north of the border (England's border, that is) comes a group of distinctive Scottish names. Some of the boys' choices, in particular, are destined for stardom.

Scottish names

G I R L S

AILSA	ISOBEL
ALEXINA	JACOBINA
AMABEL	LILIAS
AVRIL	LORNA
BEATRIX	MOIRA
BETHIA	SHEENA
ELSPETH	SHONA(H)
FENELLA	THOMASINA
GREER	

B O Y S

ALASDAIR	FERGUS
ANGUS	FRASER
ARCHIBALD	GAVIN
ARCHIE	GRAHAM
CALLUM	HAMISH
CAMPBELL	LACHLAN
CRAWFORD	MALCOLM
DUNCAN	MUNGO
EWAN	

THE IRISH

Native Irish names, popularized by singer Sinead O'Connor, actors Liam Neeson and Aidan Quinn, by Pulitzer Prize–winning novelist Cormac McCarthy, and by Letterman replacement Conan O'Brien, are due to replace overassimilated cousins Sean and Brian, Bridget and Shannon. Some Irish surname-names, à la Macauley Culkin and Murphy Brown, have already become hot, along with Waspy counterparts Cameron and Cooper and Taylor. Others, such as those listed here, or a choice from your own family, remain on the sharp side of style for boys or girls. The newest Irish immigrants include:

Irish names

G I R L S

AINE/ANYA	MAEVE
AISLING/ASHLING	MAIRE
CEARA	MAIREAD
DEIRDRE	NIAMH/NIAV
EAVAN	ORLA
FINOLA	SINEAD
FIONA	SIOBHAN
GRAINNE/GRANIA	UNA

B O Y S

AIDAN	KIERAN ✓
COLMAN ✓	KILLIAN
CONAN	LIAM
CON(N)OR	LORCAN
CONNELL	MALACHY
CORMAC	NIALL
DECLAN	OWEN (a Welsh
DEVLIN	import)
EAMON	REDMOND
FERGUS	RONAN
FINN	RORY
FIN(N)IAN	SEAMUS
FINTAN	

A M B I S E X U A L

BRADY ✓	HOGAN
BRENNAN	HUGHES
BRESLIN	KANE
CAGNEY	KEARNEY
CALHOUN	KEENAN
CALLAHAN	KIRBY
CLANCY	LENNON
COSTELLO	MAGEE
CULLEN	MAGILL
CURRAN	MALONE
DEMPSEY	NOLAN
DEVLIN	PHELAN
DOLAN	QUINLAN
DONAHUE	REYNOLDS
DONNELLY	ROURKE
FARRELL	SHERIDAN
GALLAGHER	SULLIVAN
GRADY	TIERNEY
GRIFFIN	TYNAN
HENNESSY	WHALEN

Isn't It Romantic?

Sometimes name-givers get carried away and want to preserve some especially memorable place or object forever in their child's name. Rudyard Kipling, for example, got his name from the lake where his parents courted; Mariel Hemingway was named for the Cuban bay where her parents used to fish; and Winona Ryder for a suburb of Minneapolis. Ron Howard and his wife, Cheryl, named three of their four children in commemoration of the place where they were conceived—Bryce Dallas in Dallas, and both Paige Carlyle and Jocelyn Carlyle at the Hotel Carlyle in New York.

So far out they'll Probably always be Out

We used to have a list of names here, names we considered too loaded with frumpy, dowdy, or nerdy baggage to come back into style now . . . or maybe ever. But the incredible resurgence of serious, old-fashioned names over the past five years and the determination of many parents to revive the names of their ancestors have restored many of these formerly musty names—Edna and Mildred and Franklin and Percy—to fashion prominence. Also, some famous parents, in search of an individual name for their child, looked to this list for a name no one else would ever choose. Actress Valerie Bertinelli, for instance, says she and rocker husband Eddie Van Halen named their son Wolfgang after finding it in this book under "So Far Out It Will Probably Always Be Out."

Of course, once a name is given the star seal of approval, it immediately begins the journey from out to in, and so it is with Wolfgang and many of the other names we once damned to fashion hell. In these days of hip baby girls named

Hazel and Florence and George and stylish little boys named Homer and Archie and Walter, it almost seems axiomatic that once a name is ruled out it starts to boomerang back in. Aren't some of these names still loaded with frumpy, dowdy, or nerdy baggage? Maybe. But, it seems, that's exactly the kind of name baggage that many parents consider essential.

FASHION LIMBO

There are many names that are decidedly not in, but neither are they out forever. These names—rarely chosen by contemporary parents—are in a suspended state of fashion limbo. A good many of these names were relegated to fashion limbo after being overused for and by our own parents. In fact, chances are you'll find your own name as well as your parents' names on this list.

Some of these names will undoubtedly be rediscovered by our children when they're choosing names for their babies. And we will undoubtedly be disconcerted by the idea of having grandchildren named Phyllis or Donald or Patti or Gary, just as our parents are dismayed at our own little Sams and Maxes and Rosies.

But other of these names will not fare so well (or so badly, depending on your viewpoint) and will pass into oblivion. RIP Rhoda, Myrna, Raymond, and Harold; here's hoping you don't rise again.

But wait—do we already hear some stirrings from within

this category? Sure enough, some hip, high-profile couples have already dropped into limbo land. Jack Nicholson and Rebecca Broussard named their two children Lorraine and Raymond, and Rod Stewart and Rachel Hunter have a little Renée.

G I R L S

ADELE	ETTA
ANITA	FRANCINE
ANNETTE	GAIL
ARLENE	GLADYS
AUDREY	GLORIA
BARBARA	HELENE
BERNICE	HILDA
BETSY	IRENE
BETTY	IRIS
BEVERLY	JANET
BONNIE	JANICE/JANIS
BRENDA	JEAN
CAROL	JEANETTE
CHARLENE	JOAN
DENISE	JOANNE
DIANE	JODY
DOLORES	JOY
DONNA	JOYCE
DOREEN	JUDY
DORIS	JUNE
DOROTHY	KAREN
EILEEN	LENORE
ELAINE	LINDA
ESTELLE	LISA

LOIS	PEGGY
LORETTA	PHYLLIS
LORRAINE	RENÉE
LUCILLE	RHODA
LYNN	RHONDA
MARCIA/MARSHA	RITA
MARCY	ROBERTA
MARGERY	RONA
MARJORIE	ROSALIE
MARILYN	SANDRA
MARLENE	SELMA
MAUREEN	SHARI
MAXINE	SHARON
MINDY	SHEILA
MONA	SHELLEY
MYRA	SHIRLEY
MYRNA	SONDRA
NADINE	SUSAN
NANCY	TRUDY
NANETTE	VERNA
NOREEN	WILMA
NORMA	YVETTE
PAULA	YVONNE

B O Y S

ALAN	BERTRAM
ALVIN	BRUCE
ARNOLD	BURTON
ARTHUR	CARL
BARRY	CARY
BERNARD	CLARK

CRAIG

DEAN

DENNIS

DONALD

DWAYNE

DWIGHT

EARL

EDWIN

EL(L)IOT

ERNEST

EUGENE

GARTH

GARY

GERALD

GERARD

GLENN

GRANT

HERBERT

HOWARD

IRA

IRWIN

IVAN

JAY

JEROME

JOEL

KENNETH

LANCE

LARRY

LEE

LEON

LEONARD

LESTER

MARVIN

MELVIN

MILTON

MITCHELL

NEAL/NEIL

NORMAN

RANDOLPH

RAYMOND

ROGER

RONALD

ROY

SEYMOUR

STANLEY

TERRY

TODD

TROY

VICTOR

VINCENT

WARREN

WAYNE

WILBUR

WHAT THE REST OF THE WORLD IS DOING

Style may in many ways be personal, but it's never isolated: A name's fashion status can be judged only in relation to society in general. That's why we take a look here at what the rest of the world is doing about names. You'll find lists of the most popular boys' and girls' names in the United States. You'll see what the rich and famous—often the trendsetters in all manner of style—are naming their children. And you'll get an insight into how famous names, both real and fictional, have inspired naming trends or else taken a name forever off the general market.

THE TWENTY-FIVE MOST POPULAR GIRLS' AND BOYS' NAMES IN THE UNITED STATES

For the last edition of *Beyond Jennifer & Jason*, our Most Popular list was tabulated from the statistics reported by six different states. This time, we were able to obtain figures from the Departments of Health of *thirty-five* states, making the figures more broad-based and accurate. And what new names for the nineties have entered the magic circle? Among the girls, we welcomed Kelsey, Shelby, and Hannah for the first time (replacing Tiffany, Vanessa, Whitney, and Lindsay), while the new boys on the block were Tyler (debuting at No. 9; Jordan and Alexander, supplanting Adam, José, and Benjamin). The biggest movements in the lists were Jennifer, Stephanie, Heather, and Melissa, slipping several places; Chelsea climbing from No. 23 to No. 17; Nicholas, Jacob, and Ryan moving up; Justin, Jonathan, David and Robert losing ground.

G I R L S

1. ASHLEY
2. JESSICA
3. AMANDA
4. BRITTANY
5. SARAH
6. SAMANTHA
7. MEGAN
8. EMILY
9. KAYLA
10. ELIZABETH
11. STEPHANIE
    NICOLE
13. JENNIFER

14. LAUREN
15. AMBER
16. RACHEL
17. CHELSEA
18. DANIELLE
19. COURTNEY
20. KELSEY
21. REBECCA
22. SHELBY
23. HEATHER
24. HANNAH
25. MELISSA

B O Y S

1. MICHAEL
2. CHRISTOPHER
3. JOSHUA
4. MATTHEW
5. ANDREW
6. RYAN
7. JACOB
8. NICHOLAS
9. TYLER ✓
10. JAMES
11. DANIEL
12. JOSEPH
13. JUSTIN ✓

14. DAVID
15. JOHN
16. BRANDON
17. ROBERT
18. ZACHARY
19. KYLE
20. WILLIAM
21. CODY ✓
22. ANTHONY
23. JORDAN
24. JONATHAN
25. ALEXANDER

Happy Birthday, Jennifer

I know it must be startling to realize how common your name must be for this greeting card to have been printed, but just think how much more disconcerting it would be if it also mentioned your remarkable sense of style, your love of Baroque music, your impatience with bureaucracy, and your conviction that your thighs should be thinner.

Enjoy your white wine and chocolate cake!

—Message on greeting card, Cards by Boynton

Well, the current list of favorite names for babies is out, and it's interesting to note that in the year 2057, nursing homes will be inhabited by the likes of Nicole, Megan, Lauren, Jason, Ryan, and Lindsay.

It will seem weird having a retired handyman named Ashley, a nun named Freedom and a doctor with the first name of Amiracle, but those are the current choices.

—Erma Bombeck, *Los Angeles Times* Syndicate

SECOND STRING

Although they didn't make the final cut, the following names showed strong potential in some states:

G I R L S

ALEXANDRA
ALEXIS
ALICIA
ALYSSA
ANDREA
ANNA
BRIANNA

BROOKE
CAITLIN/KAITLYN/
  CAITLYN
CASSANDRA
HAILEY/HALEY/
  HAYLEY
JASMINE

JENNA
JILLIAN
JORDAN
KATHERINE
LAURA
MARISSA
MIRANDA ✓

MOLLY
MORGAN
OLIVIA
PAIGE
TAYLOR
VICTORIA

B O Y S

AARON ✓
ADAM
AUSTIN
BENJAMIN
BRADLEY
CAMERON
COREY
DEREK
DUSTIN
DYLAN
ETHAN
EVAN ✓

GREGORY
IAN ✓
JARED ✓
LOGAN
NATHAN
PATRICK
SAMUEL
TANNER ✓
TAYLOR
TRAVIS
TREVOR

COAST TO COAST AND BEYOND

In previous editions of this book, we have pointed out the variations in baby-naming patterns across the country. And these variations do still exist. One state with a mind of its own is Utah. There the top boy's name is Jordan (number twenty-three on the national list) and the fifth most popular girl's name is the oddly spelled Kaitlyn, which isn't even on the national register. And in Arkansas, Taylor has made it to the top ten girls' list, and Morgan and Jasmine to the top twenty-five, far ahead of the rest of the country.

The bigger news, though, is not these oddities, but the startling consensus among the thirty-five states we polled. Then again, in this malled and cabled era when everyone everywhere is watching *Home Improvement* and "The Bold & the Beautiful" and shopping at parallel Gaps, electronically transmitted information of every kind zooms into every corner of the country. So should we really be surprised to find that in states as far flung as Hawaii and Alaska, seven of the top ten girls names were identical?

Cross-Cultural Notes

A few states divide their popularity lists along racial and ethnic lines, giving us some indication of what's popular among different groups. In all states studied, the No. 1 name for African-American girl babies was Jasmine, no doubt influenced by the appeal of Jasmine Guy. Briana and Kiara tied for ninth place in Delaware; Tisha, Bianca, and Dominique made strong showings in Florida, and Raven was a favorite in Texas, while Marcus and Isaiah made the boys' list. The only index to reflect African and Muslim influences and rhythms was one formulated a few years ago in Virginia, which included, for girls, Tameka, Tamika, Lakisha, Latasha, and Latoya—as well as the increasingly popular Ebony.

While some states' lists mirrored their growing Hispanic populations (California's included José and Juan in its top twenty-five), only one, Texas, had a separate Hispanic list. There, alongside Michael, Joshua, and Ashley, were found Maria, José, Juan, Jesus, Luis, and Carlos.

It's a fact. Names come "in" and go "out" again. The Johns and Marys, Barbaras and Georges, Dorothys and Charleses have enjoyed a good run. We liked them so much, we used to give our dogs human names like Harry, Kate, and Jack. I suppose now we can expect to hear, "Come on in, Brandon, I'm getting cold." "Heel, Jessica." "Stay, Melissa." "Don't drink out of the toilet, Jonathan."

—Erma Bombeck, *Los Angeles Times* Syndicate

BRIT HIT PARADE

The most popular names in England are very different from those most favored here. While a few classics—William and James, Emily and Hannah—cross over on both the British and U.S. lists, many of England's most favored names are rarely heard these days in America. But take note: Many of the more offbeat names here—Sophie, Harriet, Alice, Henry, George—may also be destined for stardom on our shores. Here, the top ten for 1992 among British parents, according to *The Times* of London:

G I R L S

1. SOPHIE
2. CHARLOTTE
3. EMILY
4. OLIVIA
5. LUCY

6. ALEXANDRA
7. HARRIET
8. HANNAH
9. ALICE
10. GEORGINA

B O Y S

1. THOMAS
2. JAMES
3. ALEXANDER
4. WILLIAM
5. OLIVER

6. GEORGE
7. CHARLES
8. EDWARD
9. HENRY
10. NICHOLAS

STAR BABIES

Their births are announced on the six o'clock news, their pictures soon appear in *People,* and their names stand a good chance of being in the public eye for the rest of their lives.

They are the children of celebrities, and the names their famous parents choose for them are the quintessence of style. Mom and Dad inhabit a glamorous and rarefied environment where being fashionable—in everything down to your child's name—is de rigueur. And if the stars aren't following fashion, they are initiating it: Unusual names can become stylish after they're chosen by even a single superstar for his or her child. Two stellar couples—Robin Wright/Sean Penn and Courtney Love/Kurt Cobain—use the name Frances for their daughters and impart an instant feeling of freshness to a dated name.

Given that, it's not surprising that the following list reads like an amalgam of the So Far Out They're In and the So Far In They're Out groups. Recent additions to the far-out side included Sting's girls Coco and Eliot Pauline, Damon Wayan's Fuddy, Jean and Casey Kasem's Liberty, Todd Rundgren's Rebop, director Jonathan Demme's Brooklyn, and Robby Benson and Karla De Vito's boy Zephyr. Funnymen Harry Anderson, Dana Carvey, and Bill Murray and their mates have come up with interesting and appropriately off-center names for their sons: Dashiell, Dex, and Homer. Hot names in Hollywood right now include Annie, Charlotte, Dakota (for both boys and girls), Taylor (ditto), Hannah, Lily, Henry, Jack, Miles, Isabelle and Isabella.

We have restricted our list to recently born children of well-known celebrities. Middle names appear when they were accessible. And finally, we do realize that none of these children arrived without both a mother and a father, and offer our apologies to those lesser-known parents who might not have received billing here.

Star Babies names

ADRIAN EDWARD ....   Edie Brickell and Paul Simon

ALESSANDRA ....   Andy Garcia

ALI (girl, twin) .... Ruth Pointer
ALYX RAY (girl) .... Faith Daniels
AMADEO.................... John Turturro
ANGUS MOORE
  (twin) .... Corbin Bernsen and
                                Amanda Pays
ANNELIESE .... Kelly Le Brock and
                                Steven Seagal
ANNIE .... Kevin Costner
ANNIE .... Jamie Lee Curtis
ANNIE MAUDE.......... Glenn Close
ARISSA .... Kelly Le Brock and
                                Steven Seagal
ASHLEY JADE .... Howard Stern
AUGUST (boy)............ Lena Olin
AUSTIN...................... Tommy Lee Jones
BEAU GRAYSON .... Tanya Tucker
BELLE KINGSTON ..... Donna Dixon and Dan
                                Ackroyd
BILLIE CATHERINE ... Carrie Fisher
BOBBI KRISTINA....... Whitney Houston and
                                Bobby Brown
BRANDON CALEB..... Richard Marx
BRAWLEY KING .... Nick Nolte
BREA .... Eddie Murphy
BROOKLYN (boy)........ Jonathan Demme
BYRON .... Mel Harris
CAIRO (girl)............... Beverly Peele
CASSIDY ERIN
  (girl) .... Kathie Lee and Frank
                                Gifford
CATHERINE CLAIRE . Crystal Gayle
CHARLOTTE.............. Sigourney Weaver
CHARLOTTE ROSE ... Rickie Lee Jones

CHESTER	Tom Hanks and Rita Wilson
CHIANNA MARIA	Sonny Bono
CHLOE	Candice Bergen and Louis Malle
CHRISTINA MARIA ..	Maria Shriver and Arnold Schwarzenegger
CLAUDIA ROSE	Michelle Pfeiffer
COCO	Sting
CODY ALAN	Robin Williams
CODY NEWTON	Kathie Lee and Frank Gifford
COLIN	Tom Hanks and Rita Wilson
CONNOR (boy, twin) ...	Ruth Pointer
COOPER	Tim Matheson
DAISY	Markie Post
DAKOTA (girl)	Melanie Griffith and Don Johnson
DAKOTA MAYI (boy) ..	Melissa Gilbert
DASHIELL	Harry Anderson
DENNI MONTANA	Woody Harrelson
DEVIN CHRISTIAN (boy)	Vanessa Williams
DEX	Dana Carvey
DOMINICK (boy)	Kelly LeBrock and Steven Seagal
DOMINIK (girl)............	Andy Garcia
DREE LOUISE	Mariel Hemingway
DYLAN FRANCES (girl)	Robin Wright and Sean Penn

EARVIN	Earvin (Magic) Johnson
ELEANOR JASMINE...	Diane Lane and Christopher Lambert
ELINOR	Katie Couric
ELIOT PAULINE.........	Sting
ELIZABETH SCARLETT..............	Jerry Hall and Mick Jagger
EMANUEL NOAH......	Debra Winger and Timothy Hutton
EMILY GRACE............	Alex Trebek
EMMA	Eric Roberts
EMMA (twin)..............	Christine Lahti
ENZO	Patricia Arquette
EVAN JAMES	Bruce Springsteen
EZEKIEL	Beau Bridges
FIFI TRIXIEBELLE.......	Bob Geldof
FRANCES BEAN (girl)	Courtney Love and Kurt Cobain
FRANCESCA RUTH FISHER	Frances Fisher and Clint Eastwood
FUDDY.......................	Daman Wayans
GARRETT..................	Bo Jackson
GEORGIA MAY..........	Jerry Hall and Mick Jagger
GRACE JANE	Meryl Streep
GRADY THOMAS......	Harry Smith
HALEY.......................	Paula Zahn
HANNAH..................	Jilly Mack and Tom Selleck
HANNAH JO.............	Elizabeth Perkins
HARRY	Richard Dreyfuss
HAYLEY ROSE...........	Jeff Bridges

HENRY........................	Dennis Hopper
HENRY........................	Julia Louis-Dreyfus and Brad Hall
HENRY PAYS (twin)....	Amanda Pays and Corbin Bernsen
HOLDEN.....................	Dennis Miller
HOMER	Bill Murray
HOPPER JACK............	Robin Wright and Sean Penn
INDIA EMMELINE.......	Marianne Williamson
INDIA RAVEN.............	Catherine Oxenberg
ISABELLA JANE KIDMAN	Nicole Kidman and Tom Cruise
ISABELLE HOLMES....	C. C. Dyer and Geraldo Rivera
JACK..........................	Ozzie Osbourne
JACK..........................	Meg Ryan and Dennis Quaid
JACK..........................	Susan Sarandon and Tim Robbins
JACK DANIEL	Ellen Barkin and Gabriel Byrne
JACKSON FREDERICK.............	Patti Smith
JAKE	Sinead O'Connor
JAMES POWELL.........	Annie Potts
JARED BRANDON	Paula Zahn
JELANI (boy)...............	Wesley Snipes
JETT (boy)...................	Kelly Preston and John Travolta
JILLIAN	Vanessa Williams
JOE............................	Kevin Costner

JOE (twin)....................	Christine Lahti
JOHN ALBERT	
VICTOR	Tracey Ullman
JOHN BOUVIER	Caroline Kennedy and
KENNEDY	Ed Schlossberg
JORDAN	
ALEXANDRA..........	Leeza Gibbons
JUSTIN	Andie MacDowell
KATHERINE	Maria Shriver
EUNICE..................	and Arnold
	Schwarzenegger
KATHLYN BENING....	Annette Bening and
	Warren Beatty
KELSEY (girl)..............	Kelly McGillis
KENYA JULIA	Nastassja Kinski and
MIAMBI SARAH.....	Quincy Jones
KERRY SOPHIA	Kathleen Kennedy and
KENNEDY	David Townsend
LANGLEY FOX (girl)...	Mariel Hemingway
LARA........................	Bob Saget
LIBERTY IRENE..........	Jean and Casey Kasem
LILY DOLORES...........	Amy Madigan and Ed
	Harris
LILY MAX..................	Meredith Viera
LOLA	Annie Lennox
LORRAINE	Rebecca Broussard and
BROUSSARD	Jack Nicholson
LOUISA JACOBSON..	Meryl Streep
LUCAS AUTRY	Willie Nelson
MABLE ELLEN............	Tracey Ullman
MADELINE	Lea Thompson
MADELINE	Mel Harris

MADISON (girl)	Sissy Spacek
MALCOLM (twin)	Denzel Washington
MALCOLM	Harrison Ford
MALLORY LOVING (girl)	Rick Derringer
MALU VALENTINE....	David Byrne
MARSTON (boy).........	Hugh Hefner
MARY WILLA.............	Meryl Streep
MATTHEW ALEXANDER	Alex Trebek
MATTHEW EDWARD	Rob Lowe
MAXWELL.................	Andrew Dice Clay
MERCEDES	Joanna Whaley-Kilmer and Val Kilmer
MILES GUTHRIE........	Susan Sarandon and Tim Robbins
MILLIE	Amy Grant
MOLLY EVANGELINE	John Goodman
MORGAN (boy)	Rae Dawn Chong
MYLES MITCHELL	Eddie Murphy
NINNA PRISCILLA	Marlon Brando
OLIVER.....................	Amanda Pays and Corbin Bernsen
OLIVER.....................	Martin Short
OLIVIA (twin)	Denzel Washington
OWEN	Christopher Reeve
OWEN JOSEPH..........	Phoebe Cates and Kevin Kline
PALOMA	Emilio Estevez
PEACHES..................	Bob Geldof
PRESLEY TANITA (girl)	Tanya Tucker

RACHEL ANN............ Kathleen Turner
RAINIE (girl).............. Andie MacDowell
RAMONA.................. Jonathan Demme
RAYMOND................ Rebecca Broussard and
Jack Nicholson
REBOP .... Todd Rundgren
REMINGTON Tracy Nelson and
ELIZABETH............ Billy Moses
RENEE .... Rod Stewart and
Rachel Hunter
RILEY PAIGE.............. Howie Mandel
ROMY MARION Ellen Barkin and
(girl)........................ Gabriel Byrne
ROSE......................... Renée Russo
ROSE KENNEDY......... Caroline Kennedy and
Ed Schlossberg
RUMER GLENN .... Demi Moore and
Bruce Willis
SADIE .... Michael Ontkean
SAM.......................... Tracy Pollan and
Michael J. Fox
SAM.......................... Sally Field
SASHA (girl) .... Kate Capshaw and
Steven Spielberg
SAVANNAH............... Jimmy Buffet
SAWYER.................... Kate Capshaw and
Steven Spielberg
SCOUT LARUE.......... Demi Moore and
Bruce Willis
SEBASTIAN................ James Spader
SHELBY STEVEN
(boy) .... Reba McEntire

SIERRA ALEXIS (girl)	(L.A. Laker) James Worthy
SONORA ASHLEY	Kelly McGillis
SOPHIE FREDERICA ALOHILANI	Bette Midler
SOSIE RUTH	Kyra Sedgwick and Kevin Bacon
STEPHANIE ROSE......	Jon Bon Jovi
TALI	Annie Lennox
TATIANA CELIA	Caroline Kennedy and Ed Schlossberg
TAYLOR LEVI (boy)....	Emilio Estevez
TAYLOR MAYNE PEARL (girl)	Garth Brooks
THOMAS....................	Dana Carvey
THEO..........................	Kate Capshaw and Steven Spielberg
TRAVIS SEDG	Kyra Sedgwick and Kevin Bacon
TRIXIE	Damon Wayans
TROY..........................	Leeza Gibbons
TY CHRISTIAN..........	Pam Dawber and Mark Harmon
TYSON (girl)	Nenah Cherry
VICTORIA..................	Tommy Lee Jones
WESTON	Nicolas Cage
WILLEM WOLF	Billy Idol
WILLIAM TRUE PARKER	Kirstie Alley and Parker Stevenson
WILSON	Christine Lahti
WOLFGANG	Valerie Bertinelli and Eddie Van Halen

WYATT	Goldie Hawn and Kurt Russell
ZACHARY	Cheryl Tiegs and Tony Peck
ZELDA	Robin Williams
ZEPHYR (boy)	Karla DeVito and Robby Benson
ZOE	Lisa Bonet and Lenny Kravitz

The Jack Pack

Baby Jacks have been sprouting up like bean-stalks. William Friedkin and Lesley-Anne Down's popped out of the box six years ago, when Willem Dafoe and Elizabeth LeCompte also hit the Jackpot. Susan Sarandon and Tim Robbins have a year-old Jack Sprat. Ellen Barkin and Gabriel Byrne had a little Jack-o-Lantern for Halloween.

—Angela Janklow, *Vanity Fair*

Much of the public believed when China [Slick, daughter of Grace] was born that her parents had named her "god." That was merely a Starship joke. As for her real name, China used to hate it. "But the more I've grown up, the more

I've begun to like it. I think me and Moon and Dweezil [Zappa, children of Frank] and Chynna [Phillips, daughter of Michelle] are a lot more fortunate than people who got names like Mary or Sue or Ted."

—*Daily News Magazine*

Bette Midler on naming her daughter Sophie: "We wanted something that would go with the European sound of my husband's name [Martin von Haselberg]. We went around Cornelia and Chloe and Zoe and all through the Brontës. We think Sophie sounds like an impoverished Austrian princess who is forced to marry a coarse member of the French bourgeoisie. He doesn't have quite her delicate upbringing, but he has piles of money. That's the story we made up for her."

—*People* magazine

GOODBYE, DICK; GOODBYE, JANE

First-time parents, largely unaware of today's unusual baby-naming trends, may well ask, "Where do you guys get this stuff?" We get it from class lists and birth announcements, from avant-garde fashions destined to trickle down to the hoi polloi and from the air. But no, that doesn't mean we make it up. For those who need hard evidence of what children are being named today, here is a roster from one hip, ethnically and culturally diverse but middle-class suburban nursery school:

G I R L S

ANNA	KRISTIANNE
ANNE	MAGGIE
ANNIE	MAYA
ASHLEY	MELISSA
CHRISTA	NINA
DAVINA	RACHAEL
EMMA	REEMA
GABRIELA	RUBY
GIOIA	SARAH
HALLIE	VALERIE
JACQUELINE	VANESSA
JORDAN	VERONICA
KELSEY	

B O Y S

ALEX (2)	EVAN (2)
ANDREW	GORDON
ARI	GRAY
AUSTIN	IAN (2)
BRANDEN	JACOB
CASEY	JEFFREY
CHAD	JEREMY
DEVIN	JOEL
ERIK	JOHN

JOSEPH	NOAH
JOSHUA	OLIVER
KARL	PETER (2)
KEIRAN	PHILLIP (2)
KONRAD	RICHARD
MARTIN	RYAN
MATHEW	SAM
MYLES	SCOTT (2)
NATHANIEL	VINCENT
NICHOLAS (2)	

THE SHIRLEY TEMPLE SYNDROME

In the early thirties, there was a sudden rise in popularity of the name Shirley, almost as meteoric as the fame of its dimpled inspiration, Shirley Temple, every mother's dream. Over the years, there have been other celebrities whose names (often not the ones they were born with) projected attractive enough images to appeal to lots of their fans when they became parents: Witness, for example, the legions of Debbies (after Reynolds), Judys (for Garland), and Garys (in honor of Cooper) born in our own generation. Unfortunately, these names can age and their popularity wane along with the celebrities who inspire them. The danger, then, of naming your child after a star is obvious: Today's fashionable little Whitney or Brooke may be tomorrow's Shirley. Our list of celebrities who are influencing current naming trends would have to include:

AIDAN Quinn	ALI (b. Alice)
ALEC (b. Alexander)	MacGraw
Baldwin	ALLY Sheedy

ALYSSA Milano
ANJELICA Huston
BEAU (b. Lloyd
Vernet) Bridges
BLAIR Brown
BROOKE (b. Christa
Brooke) Shields
CANDICE Bergen
CARLY Simon
DANIELLE Steele
DELTA Burke
DREW Barrymore
DUSTIN Hoffman
Bob DYLAN
(b. Robert
Zimmerman) &
DYLAN Thomas
GARTH Brooks
HARRISON Ford

JASMINE Guy
JERMAINE Jackson
JODIE (b. Alicia)
Foster
JUSTINE Bateman
KIRK Cameron
KIRSTIE Alley
KYLE MacLachlan
LATOYA Jackson
LINDSAY Wagner
MARIAH Carey
MIRANDA Richardson
MIA (b. Maria) Farrow
MORGAN (b. Patsy)
Fairchild
RAVEN Simone
TIFFANY
VANESSA Redgrave
WHITNEY Houston

Other names, such as DARYL Hannah and GLENN Close, while not being used much themselves, are having the indirect influence of making male names more popular for girls.

STAR-SANCTIONED NAMES

When Brooke Shields confided to us about her Calvins, we all knew who (and what) she was talking about. While Calvin Klein may have made his name famous, it's not linked to his persona with iron chains, the way names like Thelonius and Tennessee (see "There's Only One Arsenio," page 81) are bound to their sole owners. What we're saying is that the star-sanctioned names that follow are all viable options: There's no reason you can't have a little Calvin (or Flannery or Paloma) of your own.

ARLO Guthrie
ANDIE MacDowell
BERNADETTE Peters
BIANCA Jagger
BLYTHE Danner ✓
BO (b. Mary Cathleen)
    Derek
BRONSON Pinchot
CALVIN Klein
CAMPBELL Scott
CICELY Tyson
CORETTA Scott King
CRISPIN Glover
DASHIELL (b. Samuel
    Dashiell) Hammett
DINAH (b. Frances)
    Shore
DIXIE Carter
DUDLEY Moore
ELIJAH Wood
ELLE MacPherson
FARRAH (b. Mary
    Farrah) Fawcett
HALLE Berry
IONE Skye
JACKSON Browne

KADEEM Hardison
KELSEY Grammer
KESHIA Knight-
    Pulliam
KYRA Sedgwick
LARA Flynn Boyle
LIAM Neeson
LEVAR Burton
LOLITA Davidovich
LORENZO Lamas
MARIEL Hemingway
MARLEE Matlin
MARLO (b. Margaret
    Julia) Thomas
MARLON Brando
MAYA Angelou
MELBA (b. Beatrice)
    Moore
MERYL (b. Mary
    Louise) Streep
NASTASSJA (b.
    Natassja) Kinski
NICOLETTE Sheridan
PALOMA Picasso
PIPER (b. Rosetta)
    Laurie

PRISCILLA Presley
QUINCY Jones
RAIN Pryor
RAQUEL Welch
ROONE Arledge
SADIE Frost
SHEENA Easton
TIA Carrere
TALIA Shire

TATUM O'Neal
TEMPESTT Bledsoe
TYNE (b. Ellen Tyne)
   Daly
WILLEM (b. William)
   Dafoe
WINONA Ryder
WYNTON Marsalis

THERE'S ONLY ONE ARSENIO

And only one Elton, Sigourney, Tuesday, and all the other names listed here. What we're trying to tell you is that there is not room in this world for two; these names are taken. Giving one to your child is like sentencing her to a lifetime of saying, for instance, "Yes, as in Sonny and . . ." These one-person names include:

ADLAI Stevenson
ADOLF (the classic
   case) Hitler
ALFRE WOODARD
ANAÏS Nin
ARETHA Franklin
ARSENIO Hall
AYN Rand
CHAKA Khan
CHARLTON
   Heston
CHASTITY Bono

CHER (b. Cherilyn)
CHEVY (b. Cornelius
   Crane) Chase
COKIE Roberts
CONWAY (b. Harold)
   Twitty
CORBIN Bernsen
CUBA Gooding, Jr.
DABNEY Coleman
DEMI (Demetria)
   Moore
DENZEL Washington

DESI (Desiderio) Arnaz
(Sr. and Jr.)
EARTHA Kitt
EERO Saarinen
ELDRIDGE (b.
Leroy Eldridge)
Cleaver
ELTON (b. Reginald)
John
ELVIS Presley
EMO Phillips
ENGLEBERT
(b. Arnold)
Humperdinck
ENYA
FESS Parker
FISHER Stevens
GORE (b. Eugene)
Vidal
HUME Cronyn
HUMPHREY
Bogart
IMAN
JUDGE (b. Edward)
Reinhold
JUICE (b. Judy)
Newton
KEANU Reeves
KEIR Dullea
KIEFER Sutherland
LEVAR (b. Levardis)
Burton

LEONTYNE (b. Mary)
Price
MACAULEY Culkin
MADONNA (b. Louise
Ciccone)
MAHALIA Jackson
MARE Winningham
MARKIE Post
MAYIM Bialik
MENASCH Taylor
MERCE Cunningham
MERLIN Olsen
MONTEL Williams
NENEH Cherry
OLYMPIA Dukakis
ORAL Roberts
ORNETTE Coleman
PARK Overall
PAULY Shore
REGIS Philbin
RIDDICK Bowe
ROCK (b. Roy) Hudson
RUE (b. Eddi-Rue)
McClanahan
RUSH Limbaugh
SADE (b. Helen)
SEASON Hubley
SHADOE (b. Terry)
Stevens
SHAQUILLE O'Neal
SIGOURNEY (b.
Susan) Weaver

SINBAD
SPALDING Gray
STOCKARD Channing
STONE Phillips
STROM Thurmond
SWOOSIE Kurtz
TAI Babilonia
TALLULAH Bankhead
TENNESSEE (b.
Thomas) Williams
THELONIUS Monk
THURGOOD Marshall
TIPPER (b. Mary
Elizabeth) Gore
TREAT Williams
TRUMAN Capote
TUESDAY (b. Susan)
Weld

TWYLA Tharp
UMA Thurman (a Hindu
name chosen by her
father, who teaches
Eastern religions)
VANNA White
VIDAL Sassoon
WAYLON Jennings
WHOOPI (b. Caryn)
Goldberg
WINGS Hauser
WYNTON Marsalis
YAPHET Kotto
YEARDLEY Smith
YUL (b. Taidje)
Brynner
ZERO (b. Samuel)
Mostel

When Annie Hall was pregnant, she once sat next to a man on an airplane who asked if she had thought of a name for her baby and, pointing to a page of the book he was reading, suggested Arsenio. A few months later, when she spotted the name on her own, she took that as an omen, and bestowed it on her only child.

—"Late Night Cool" by Michael Norman, *The New York Times Magazine*

There have also been fictional characters whom we all see as the quintessence of some quality—usually either stark black or white—to the point where what they are called becomes more totem than name. Ebenezer, for example, will always represent a bah, humbug! mentality, Cinderella will eternally wear a glass slipper, and Kermit will be forever green.

Other cases in point:

L'il ABNER
ALVIN and the
   Chipmunks
BARBIE Doll
BARNEY the Purple
   Dinosaur
BART Simpson
CASPER the Friendly
   Ghost
CINDERELLA
CLARABELL the
   clown
CONAN the Barbarian
EBENEZER Scrooge
ELMER Fudd
ELSIE the cow
FERDINAND the
   bull
GARFIELD the cat
GOMER Pyle
GROVER on Sesame
   Street

HANNIBAL "the
   Cannibal" Lecter
IAGO
ICHABOD Crane
KERMIT the Frog
LINUS
LOLITA
Little LULU
MAYNARD G. Krebs
MYRTLE the turtle
OLIVE Oyl
OPHELIA
OSCAR the Grouch
POLLYANNA
RHETT Butler
RUDOLPH the Red-
   nosed Reindeer
SCARLETT O'Hara
SHERLOCK Holmes
TINKERBELL
URIAH Heep
WINNIE the Pooh

NEU SPELLINGS

The creative spellings of these celebrities' names have, for better or worse, become accepted alternatives. If you're tempted to follow suit and spell your child's name in an original way, check the dangers in "Catherine, Katharine, and Kathrynne," page 213.

ANN-MARGRET
AXL ROSE
BARBRA Streisand
CHYNNA Philips
CYBILL Shepherd
CYNDI Lauper
DAWNN Lewis
DIAHANN (b. Carol
  Diahann) Carroll
DYAN Cannon
EFREM Zimbalist
  (Jr. and Sr.)
ELAYNE Boosler
EVONNE Goolagong
GEENA (b. Virginia)
  Davis
GENNIFER Flowers
JACKEE Harry
JACLYN Smith
JAYNE (b. Vera Jane)
  Mansfield
JERMAINE Jackson
JESSYE Norman
JIMI (b. Johnny Allen)
  Hendrix
JONI (b. Roberta Joan)
  Mitchell
KHRYSTYNE Haye
LEEZA Gibbons
MARGAUX
  Hemingway
PHYLICIA Rashaad
SHANNEN DOHERTY
STEFANIE (b. Stefania
  Zofia) Powers
STEPFANIE Kramer
WYNONNA (b.
  Christina) Judd

Just Inn from Idahoe

Spelling creativity reigns in the potatoe capital. In 1991, the state's Cooperative Center for Health Statistics reported that its records showed eighteen different spellings for the name Brittany and fourteen for Zachary. Other oddities included Aubirhnn, Rumour, and Jake-Cob, not to mention girls named Charm, Feather, Meadow, September, Jovanique, Shouston, and Twinkle, and baby boys greeting the world as Bach, J2, Taylorbud, Titan, and Thorbjorn.

ELECTRONIC INSPIRATION

There is little doubt that movies and television—TV in particular—have had considerable influence on naming patterns. Sometimes the effect has been immediate; often it becomes evident when the generation who watched certain popular shows as children and adolescents reaches child-bearing age.

The Westerns and hillbilly shows that rode the airwaves in the late fifties and through the sixties, for example, led to the hordes of city cowboys in the playgrounds of the seventies, to wit:

ADAM	"Bonanza"
BARNABY	"Wagon Train"

BART	"Maverick"
BEAU	"Wells Fargo, Maverick"
BEN	"Bonanza"
BRENT	"Maverick"
BRET	"Maverick"
CHEYENNE	"Cheyenne"
FLINT	"Wagon Train"
JARROD	"Big Valley"
JASON	"Wanted: Dead or Alive, Here Come the Brides"
JEB	"Wells Fargo"
JED	"Rawhide, How the West Was Won"
JEREMY	"Here Come the Brides"
JOSH	"Wanted: Dead or Alive"
JOSHUA	"Here Come the Brides"
LUCAS	"Rifleman"
LUKE	"How the West Was Won"
MATT	"Gunsmoke"
SETH	"Wagon Train"
SIMON	"Rawhide"
ZEB	"How the West Was Won"

SUDSY SOURCES

With some few exceptions, such as "Murphy Brown," sitcoms, dramatic and adventure shows have always been populated with mainstream-named characters—lots of Mikes and Maggies and Dans and Dianes. But the genre that has taken over the reins from the old Westerns is, without question, the soap opera. It's almost inevitable these days that when a name suddenly leaps onto popularity charts nationwide, seemingly out of nowhere, we find the genesis of the phenomenon in a soap opera character. In the recent past, such names as Ashley, Amanda, Brittany, Jordan, Lindsay, and Tiffany were all soap staples long before they were commonly seen on birth announcements.

The supreme example of the influence of soap opera on American nomenclature is the name Kayla. When the character Kayla Brady was introduced on "Days of Our Lives" in 1982, you would have been hard-pressed to find Kayla in any baby-naming guides. And yet, in 1986, with absolutely no other visible means of support, it had become among the top forty names in several states, and has continued to climb ever since. Last year it was number nine on the national list, and as high as fourth place in some states, such as Alabama.

Two other names have followed this pattern, jumping off the TV screen and onto baby bracelets: Kelsey ("Another World") and Shelby ("Loving")—both girls' names, in case you were wondering. In the wink of an eye, Kelsey has vaulted to as high as number nine (in Idaho), and Shelby is in eighth place in Kansas.

Below is a list of soap names that could take off just as precipitously; those that have already had an influence are starred.

F E M A L E

AMANDA*	"Another World"
ANGEL	"As the World Turns"
ARIEL	"As the World Turns"
ASHLEY*	"The Young and the Restless"
BIANCA	"All My Children"
BLAKE	"Guiding Light"
BRITTANY*	"Another World"
CALLA	"Guiding Light"
CAMILLE	"The Bold and the Beautiful"
CARLY*	"Days of Our Lives"
CHELSEA*	"Guiding Light"
CLOVER	"One Life to Live"
CONNOR	"As the World Turns"
COURTNEY*	"As the World Turns"/ "One Life to Live"
CRICKET	"The Young and the Restless"
DAISY	"All My Children"
DELILAH	"One Life to Live"
DEVON	"All My Children"
DINAH	"Loving"
DIXIE	"All My Children"
DOMINIQUE	"General Hospital"
DORIAN	"One Life to Live"
DRUCILLA	"The Young and the Restless"
DYLAN*	"Santa Barbara"

EDWINA	"As the World Turns"/ "One Life to Live"
EGYPT	"Loving"
GWYNETH	"Loving"
HANNAH*	"Loving"
HARLEY	"Guiding Light"
HAYLEY*	"All My Children"
HILARY	"The Young and the Restless"/"Guiding Light"
INDIA	"Guiding Light"
ISABELLE*	"Loving"
JADE	"As the World Turns"/ "General Hospital"
JENNA*	"Guiding Light"/ "Another World"
KAT	"Guiding Light"
KAYLA*	"Days of Our Lives"
KENDALL	"All My Children"
KELSEY*	"Another World"
LAUREL	"Another World"
LILY	"As the World Turns"
LINDSAY*	"Loving"
LIVIA	"All My Children"
LUCINDA	"As the World Turns"
LUNA	"One Life to Live"
MACY	"The Bold and the Beautiful"
MARGO	"As the World Turns"
MARLEY	"Another World"
NEAL	"As the World Turns"

OLIVIA*   "The Young and the Restless"/"General Hospital"/"As the World Turns"

PAULINA   "Another World"

SAMI   "Days of Our Lives"

SAVANNAH*   "Days of Our Lives"

SHELBY*   "Loving"

SIERRA   "As the World Turns"

SILVER   "All My Children"

SKYE   "All My Children"

SUMMER   "Santa Barbara"

TAYLOR*   "The Bold and the Beautiful"/"All My Children"/"As The World Turns"

TIFFANY*   "General Hospital"

M A L E

AUSTIN*   "Days of Our Lives"/ "Loving"

BO   "Days of Our Lives"

BRANDON   "Guiding Light"/ "All My Children"

CAIN   "One Life to Live"

CALEB   "As The World Turns"

CAMERON*   "General Hospital"/ "Guiding Light"

CLAY   "Guiding Light"/"Loving"

CONNOR*   "General Hospital"/"The Bold and the Beautiful"

COOPER	"Loving"
CORD	"One Life to Live"
DEREK	"All My Children"/ "General Hospital"/ "Guiding Light"
DESMOND	"Loving"
DIMITRI	"All My Children"
DUNCAN*	"As the World Turns"
DUSTIN*	"As the World Turns"
DYLAN*	"Guiding Light"
FINIAN	"General Hospital"
FLETCHER	"Guiding Light"
FRISCO	"General Hospital"
GILES	"One Life to Live"
HARLAN	"General Hospital"
HART	"Guiding Light"/"Days of Our Lives"
HOLDEN	"As the World Turns"
HUNTER	"One Life to Live"
IAN*	"Another World"
JACKSON	"All My Children"/ "Guiding Light"
JAGGER	"General Hospital"
JARED*	"The Young and the Restless"
JUSTIN*	"Guiding Light"
LARS	"All My Children"
LEO*	"Loving"
LOGAN*	"Guiding Light"
LUCAS	"Another World"/"All My Children"/"Days of Our Lives"

MAX	"One Life to Live"
RIDGE	"The Bold and the Beautiful"
RIO	"Loving"
SPENCER	"Another World"
TANNER*	"Days of Our Lives"
TRAVIS*	"All My Children"
TREVOR*	"All My Children"
TUCKER	"As the World Turns"
WYATT	"All My Children"

Soap Names

"In the 60s, the idea was to make soap opera character names as everyday as possible," says Douglas Marland, head writer for 'As the World Turns.' "Now it's like a contest to see who can come up with the most unusual names." Although Marland prefers traditional names, his show is no laggard, with Courtney, Connor, Iva, Ambrose, Caleb, and Linc, among others.

Those silly monikers help tell the story, says Bill Bell, who shepherds both "The Bold and the Beautiful" and "The Young and the Restless." A name is befitting of the character. "You're building a portrait," says Bell, whose B&B features Thorne, Ridge, Cricket, and Brooke.

"We take a tremendous amount of time to come up with the right name, long after we've worked out the background and we know where they're going," says Marland. ATWT has a true-blue, patriotic family, with Woody for Woodrow, and Linc, for Lincoln; a farm family whose salt-of-the-earth women are called Iva, Ellie and Meg; and a young man battered by fate and "searching for himself," whose name is Holden. Apologies to J.D.

—Edward Silver, *Los Angeles Times Magazine*

In March 1987, CBS introduced a new soap opera called "The Bold and the Beautiful." Among the leading male characters were a Ridge, a Thorn, and a Storm. Said John J. O'Connor in his *New York Times* review: "If nothing else, the names concocted for their characters are alone worth dipping into 'The Bold and the Beautiful' for a hoot or two."

MUCH ADO ABOUT NAMING

William Shakespeare drew upon Holinshead's *Chronicles* and Plutarch's *Lives* and Boccaccio's *Decameron* as sources of inspiration. Now it's our turn to draw upon his characters' names. Some of the most attractive:

F E M A L E

ADRIANA   *The Comedy of Errors*
ARIEL   *The Tempest*
BEATRICE   *Much Ado About Nothing*
BIANCA   *The Taming of the Shrew, Othello*
CASSANDRA   *Troilus and Cressida*
CELIA   *As You Like It*
CHARMIAN   *Antony and Cleopatra*
CORDELIA   *King Lear*
CRESSIDA   *Troilus and Cressida*
DESDEMONA   *Othello*
DIANA   *All's Well That Ends Well*
DORCAS   *The Winter's Tale*
EMILIA   *Othello, The Winter's Tale*
HELENA   *A Midsummer Night's Dream, All's Well That Ends Well*
IMOGEN   *Cymbeline*
ISABEL   *Henry V*
ISABELLA   *Measure for Measure*
JACQUENETTA   *Love's Labour's Lost*
JESSICA   *The Merchant of Venice*
JULIA   *Two Gentlemen of Verona*
JULIET   *Romeo and Juliet*
JUNO   *The Tempest*
LAVINIA   *Titus Andronicus*
LUCIANA   *The Comedy of Errors*
MARINA   *Pericles*
MIRANDA   *The Tempest*
NERISSA   *The Merchant of Venice*
OCTAVIA   *Antony and Cleopatra*
OLIVIA   *Twelfth Night*
OPHELIA   *Hamlet*

PAULINA   *The Winter's Tale*
PHEBE   *As You Like It*
PORTIA   *The Merchant of Venice, Julius Caesar*
REGAN   *King Lear*
ROSALIND   *As You Like It*
ROSALINE   *Love's Labour's Lost*
TAMORA   *Titus Andronicus*
TITANIA   *A Midsummer Night's Dream*
VIOLA   *Twelfth Night*

M A L E

ADRIAN   *The Tempest*
ALONSO   *The Tempest*
ANGUS   *Macbeth*
ANTONIO   *The Tempest, Two Gentlemen of Verona, Merchant of Venice, Much Ado About Nothing*
BALTHASAR   *Romeo and Juliet, Merchant of Venice, Much Ado About Nothing*
BALTHAZAR   *A Comedy of Errors*
BENEDICK   *Much Ado About Nothing*
CLAUDIO   *Measure for Measure, Much Ado About Nothing*
CLEON   *Pericles*
CORIN   *As You Like It*
CORNELIUS   *Hamlet*
DION   *The Winter's Tale*
DUNCAN   *Macbeth*
FABIAN   *Twelfth Night*
FRANCISCO   *Hamlet*
GREGORY   *Romeo and Juliet*
HORATIO   *Hamlet*
HUMPHREY   *Henry VI, Part II*

LORENZO   *The Merchant of Venice*
LUCIUS   *Timon of Athens, Titus Andronicus, Julius Caesar*
MALCOLM   *Macbeth*
OLIVER   *As You Like It*
ORLANDO   *As You Like It*
OWEN   *Henry IV, Part I*
PHILO   *Antony and Cleopatra*
SAMPSON   *Romeo and Juliet*
SEBASTIAN   *Twelfth Night, The Tempest*
TIMON   *Measure for Measure*
TOBY   *Twelfth Night*

Comical Names

Creators of cartoons and comic strips often offer their own droll perspective on the name game. Some of the better examples we've spotted:

   *Woman lying in bed: "I dreamt the president asked me to sacrifice something to shrink the deficit and I suggested guys with funny first names—Newt, Strom, Rush . . ."

—*Sylvia* by Nicole Hollander

*Woman to man: "I think I'm a pretty average Jennifer—but I think you're a very unusual Scott."

—William Hamilton, in *The New Yorker*

*Dialogue between two women on park bench: "So what's your son's name?"

"Jeff."

"You call him Jeffrey, I hope. Our child is named Christopher, but we wouldn't *dream* of calling him Chris!"

"Jeff's a little boy. Nicknames are easier. And, some might add, a tad less pretentious."

"Now, Joan . . . it's Joan, isn't it?"

"Joanie."

—*Doonesbury* by Garry Trudeau

*One dog to another: "For the girls—Kimberly, Caitlin, Lauren, Cindy, and Tracy. For the boys—Cameron, Christopher, Adam, Jeffrey, and Gregory."

—Leo Cullum, in *The New Yorker*

*Father and daughter looking at family album: "Great-grandpa Farnum Flagston married Bumby Wagstaff. Their kids were Mopsy, Weezy and Otie. Grandpa and Grandma had Baba, Tinker and me, Hiram. Then came Chip, you and Ditto, and Trixie."

Eavesdropping son: "I'm gonna name *my* kids Jim, John, Mary and Sue!"

—*Hi and Lois* by Brian and Greg Walker

*Little girl to mom: "Let's go crosstown. This playground has too many other Samanthas."

—P. Relly, in *The New Yorker*

IMAGE

As his name is, so is he.

—Samuel, XXV, 25

Every name sends out signals even before it's attached to a specific physical presence. It transmits subliminal messages and reverberations of its own: a level of energy, an intensity of color and sheen, a texture.

The image of the name you choose will precede your child throughout his or her lifetime. Strangers will use it as the basis for making certain assumptions about him or her: as someone intellectual or physical, attractive or plain, well-born or plebeian, unique or one of the crowd. Of course, your child's personality and presence will be the real determining factors in other people's judgments, but the power of a name to spur unconscious expectations is not to be underestimated.

The first names we will examine in this section are the ones we call the Power Names—those that conjure up someone smart or creative or energetic. The names in each of these three Power groups are distinct in tone and style, and your preference for one or the other will probably be clear, depending on your own hopes for your child's persona and talents.

Names can also project a physical image, not just of a person's attractiveness, but of the particular brand of appeal: sexy or pretty, refined or roguish. The force of names on people's perceptions of another's looks is well documented by studies outlined here, together with lists of names that have an attractive image.

Class is also an issue, albeit a touchy one, when it comes to a name's image. At any given time, some names are moving up the social ladder, improving their class standing, while others are moving down. Here you'll find today's upwardly mobile names, those that in the future can give your child a classy image.

Another image consideration is your child's position vis à vis his peers, how much his name will set him apart from the crowd or make him one of the gang. It's not difficult to pick the names at either extreme, but it's harder to define those that will help your child fit in and stand out. That's the list we present here. If you want to give your child an unusual name, will it help or harm him? We'll look at what psychologists have discovered about that. You'll also find a guide to names with images that may seem either too much or too little for a child to live up to.

And if the whole idea of a name's image defining your child appalls you, we offer here a selection of No Image names: those that have been used so frequently by such diverse groups of people that they present no clearly defined image of their own.

As the name Susie seemed too prim for a six-footer, she rechristened herself Sigourney, a name that she'd found in *The Great Gatsby*. Her father tried to persuade her to drop this affectation, pointing out that it was a man's name and that she was mispronouncing it to boot: "It is SIGourney, not SiGOURney." But she refused to budge.

—*Premiere* magazine

If your baby is a redhead, or you're hoping it will be, you may want to consider these names that mean red:

BAYARD	ROWAN/ROHAN
REED/READ/REID	ROY
ROONEY	RUFUS
RORY	RUSKIN
ROSS	RUSSELL

POWER NAMES

The power of a name is often quite specific. Many strongly suggest a person who is particularly smart or energetic or creative. We have singled these out and call them the Power Names. Whether it is Intellectual Power, Creative Power, or High Energy, each has a potent image that can work for—or against—your child throughout his or her lifetime.

Some of this power comes from stereotypes: Martha the serious student and Bonnie the bouncy cheerleader. Sound also plays a part in imbuing names with power: Short, clipped names tend to suggest efficiency, for instance, while exotic or foreign names can have a creative, even a sexy ring.

Often, however, a name's power is drawn from more mysterious sources. But whatever its root, the image is unmistakeable. If you're in doubt, consider this: Of Helen, Kirstie, and Ariadne, who is the professor, who the gymnast, who the poet? While a Helen may very well do handsprings, a Kirstie lecture at Harvard, and an Ariadne negotiate loans, each will always be battling the image of her name.

Power names can be self-fulfilling prophecies. This is not because of some cabalistic force inherent in the name, but because it was chosen by parents who identify with the image the name projects. A painter and an actress, for instance, may prefer a name like Ariadne, with its creative undertones, over the kinetic Kirstie or the intellectual Helen for their child. Ariadne grows up in a house filled with her father's paintings, sees her mother perform on the stage, associates with the children of her parents' creative friends; is nurtured, in short, in a creative atmosphere. With that kind of background, she is likely to have a creative bent, no matter what her name.

Of course, naming your child Ariadne will not automatically make her creative. Power names say more about parents' expectations than they do about a child's talents. A child who has a different kind of power than her name suggests—the Ariadne who wants to grow up to be a businesswoman, or a gymnast—may feel, each time she says her name, that she is not what her parents hoped she would be. On the other hand, a power name can add dimension to one's personality with no effort on the part of its bearer. The numbers-crunching Ariadne, for instance, may enjoy being imagined "artistic" without ever having to set foot in a museum.

For their potential bonuses as well as burdens, you would do well to consider the following lists when choosing a name for your child.

INTELLECTUAL POWER NAMES

Names with Intellectual Power suggest someone who is not only intelligent but serious and studious.

The good news for these Intellectual Power names is that many are new arrivals on the fashion scene, which may actually be enough to make it cool to sound smart. Add twenty points to estimates of your child's IQ by naming her or him:

G I R L S

ABIGAIL	HARRIET
ADELE	HELEN
ALICE	HONOR
ANNA	HOPE
BEATRICE	IRENE
BERNICE	JUDITH
CATHERINE/	JULIA
KATHERINE	KAY
CHARLOTTE	LENORE
CLAIRE	LOUISE
CLAUDIA	MADEL(E)INE
CLORIS	MARGARET
CONSTANCE	MARIAN
CORA	MARTHA
DOROTHY	MATILDA
EDITH	MIRIAM
ELEANOR	NATALIE
ESTHER	NORA
EVE	NORMA
FAITH	PAULA
FLORENCE	PHILIPPA
FRANCES	PRUDENCE
GILLIAN	ROSALIND
GRACE	RUTH

SYDNEY

VIRGINIA

SYLVIA

VIVIAN

THEODORA

WINIFRED

B O Y S

ADLAI

LINCOLN

ALBERT

MARSHALL

ARTHUR

MAXWELL

AUGUSTUS

MORTON

BYRON

NATHAN

CHARLES

NELSON

CLIVE

NORMAN

CONRAD

OWEN

CYRIL

PAUL

DREW

PHIL(L)IP

EL(L)IOT

QUINCY

FRANKLIN

RUPERT

GILBERT

SAUL

GORDON

SOLOMON

HAROLD

SPENCER

HENRY

STUART/STEWART

HOWARD

THEODORE

HUGH

TRUMAN

LAWRENCE

WALTER

LEONARD

WINSTON

Sorry, Dawn, But Doris Got the Job

Sexy is not powerful, at least when it comes to a name that will get your daughter a good job. So suggests a master's thesis written by Deborah Linville while at Rensselaer Polytechnic Institute, which compared the relationship between "sexy" names and corporate hiring. Linville's conclusion: "The present study indicates that there is a prejudice regarding women applicants based on the degree of sexiness of their first names."

Names considered too sexy for executives, according to Linville's study, are: Adrienne, Andrea, Cheryl, Christine, Dawn, Erica, Heather, Jennifer, and Kathy. Names destined for corporate success include Alma, Cornelia, Doris, Ethel, Mildred, and Zelda.

CREATIVE POWER NAMES

Creative Power names tend to display a certain amount of creativity on the part of their bestowers: They are often unusual, exotic, sometimes foreign-sounding, sometimes associated with an artistic figure. Pablo sounds more creative than Pedro simply because of Picasso. Names with Creative Power set your child apart from the herd; from the beginning, he or she is seen as someone special. Any one of those listed here would not look out of place on a theater marquee or a book jacket, in a dance program or a gallery guide. Encourage your child's creativity with a name like:

G I R L S

ABRA	CHINA
ADRIA(NA)	CHLOE
ALEXA	CLEA
ALLEGRA	CLEMENTINE
ANAIS	CLIO/CLEO
ANDRA	COLETTE
ANABEL	COLUMBINE
ANTHEA	DAISY
ARABELLA	DALLAS
ARDITH	DAPHNE
ARIADNE	DARIA
ARIEL	DARYL
ASTRA	DEIRDRE
AUDRA	DELIA
AURORA/AURELIA	DEVON
BARRA	DIANTHA
BETHANY	DINAH
BIANCA	DOMINIQUE
BLYTHE	DORIAN
BREE	DYLAN
BRONWYN/	ELECTRA
BRONWEN	ESMÉ
BRYN	EVANGELINE
CAMILLE/CAMILLA	FELICITY
CANDIDA	FEODORA
CASSANDRA	FLANNERY

FLAVIA
FLEUR
FRANCESCA
GABRIELLE/GABRIELLA
GELSEY
GEMMA
GENEVA
GEORGIA(NA)
GERMAINE
GISELLE
GREER
GWYN/GWYNETH
ILANA/ILIANA
INDIA
IONE
ISA
ISABEL(LA)
ISADORA
IVY
JADE
JAEL
JASMINE
JESSAMINE
JUSTINE
KAIA
KAYLA/KAILA
KEISHA
KEZIA(H)
KYLE
KYRA
LALLY
LARA

LEATRICE
LEILA
LELIA
LEONIE
LEYA
LIANA
LILIANA
LILITH
LILO
LILY
LOLA
LUCIANA
LULU
MACKENZIE
MAIA
MALA
MARA
MARGAUX
MARIEL
MARIS(S)A
MARLO
MARYA
MAUD(E)
MERCEDES
MICHAEL/MICHAELA
MINTA
MIRABEL
MIRANDA
MIRRA
NADIA
NATASHA/NASTASSIA
NEDDA

NESSA
NEVA
NICOLA
ODELIA
ODETTE
OLIVIA
OPHELIA
ORIANA
OUIDA
PALOMA
PERRY
PETRA
PHILIPPA
PHOEBE
PILAR
PORTIA
QUINTANA/QUINTINA
RAFFAELA
REINE
RENATA
RHEA/RIA
SABINE
SABRA
SACHA/SASHA
SAVANNAH
SCARLETT
SHANA

SHOSHANA
SILVER
SIMONE
SKYE
SOPHIA
SYDNEY
TALIA
TALLULAH
TAMAR(A)
TANYA
TATIANA
TESS(A)
TRILBY
TWYLA
TYNE
VALENTINA
VENICE/VENETIA
VIOLET
WALKER
WILLA
WYNN(E)
ZANDRA
ZANE
ZARA
ZELIA
ZOE

B O Y S

ADRIAN
ALEXIS

ALISTAIR
AMYAS

ANATOL
ANDRÉ/ANDREAS
ANTON
BASIL
BEAU
BENNO
BOAZ
BORIS
CALEB
CHRISTO
CLAY
CLEMENT
CLOVIS
CODY
COLE
COSMO
CRISPIN
DALLAS
DARIUS
D(I)MITRI
DION
DORIAN
DYLAN
EBEN
ELIAS
ELISHA
ELLERY
EMMETT
EPHRAIM
EZRA
GABRIEL
GARSON

GIDEON
GRAY/GREY
HART
INIGO
JAMESON
JARED
JASPER
JEREMIAS
JETHRO
JONAH
JOSIAH
JULIAN
KAI
KELSEY
KENYON
KILIAN
LIAM
LIONEL
LONDON
LORENZO
LORNE
LUCIAN
MACKENZIE
MARCO
MARCUS
MARIUS
MERCE(R)
MICAH
MILO
MISCHA
MOSES
MOSS

NATHANIEL
NICO
NOAH
OMAR
ORLANDO
ORSON
PABLO
PHILO
PHINEAS
QUENTIN

RAFAEL
RAOUL
ROBIN
SEBASTIAN
SIMON
SKY
THADDEUS
THEO
TOBIAS
TRISTAN

Creative class

Bennington College has long had the reputation of being a hotbed of creative activity. The following partial list of names of students, both male and female, enrolled there during a recent school year certainly reflects the creative activity of their parents during the naming process.

AMER
AMINA
ANDERS
ANGHELIKA
ARIANE
ARIELE
ARJUN
ARNIS
AURA
BARNABAS
BERIL
BRENNA
BRYN

CHIARA
CIARAN
DANIELIA
DECLAN
DESIRÉE
EMORY
FAIZA
FAYNE
FELICITY
FLANNERY
GHAZI
GIBBS
GIOIA

HYLA	MERILEE
IOANNIS	MIRI
ITALIA	MOLLIA
JOVITA	PARRISH
KAIJA	PIPER
KALEB	RAFE
KHEYA	RHODY
LARA	RIO
LARISSA	RUSHA
LELLA	SAVO
LIMORE	SCHUYLER
LORELIE	SEKKA
LYNMORE	SHONA
MACEY	SIMEON
MAIYA	TAMAR
MANAL	TAMARA
MARYA	VEENA
MAYA	ZARAAWAR
MERCEDES	

HIGH-ENERGY NAMES

Names with physical power—High-Energy names—fairly cartwheel off the tongue, conjuring up a person in constant motion. A disproportionate number of these names end in a long *e* sound, consistent with adjectives like bouncy and perky. At their peak in the early sixties—during JFK's "vigor" administration—many High Energy names will still serve a child well. You should be aware, however, that there is energy and then there's energy: the competent grown-up kind suggested by names like Jill and Brady, and the pep-squad teenager variety personified by such names as Cindy and

Tammy and Jamie, which often prove not enough to live up to. The difference between the two groups is readily apparent, and if you want a supercharged image of either kind, consider the following:

G I R L S

AILEEN	JAN
ALI/ALLY/ALLIE	JILL
AMY	JO
ANNIE	JODY
BARBIE	JOLIE
BETSY	JOY
BONNIE	JULIE
CAREY/CARRIE	KEELY
CARLY	KELLY
CASEY	KELSEY
CHRISTIE	KERRY
CINDY	KIM
DEBBIE	KIRSTIE
DENA	LAURIE
DIXIE	LEXIE
DOLLY	LINDA
EILEEN	LISA
ERIN	LUCY
GAIL	MARCY
GAY	MELODY
GINNY	MERRY
GOLDIE	MIMI
HEIDI	MINDY
HOLLY	MITZI
JAMIE	PATSY

PATTY	SHELL(E)Y
PEGGY	SHERRY
PENNY	STACEY
PEPPER	TAFFY
PIPER	TAI
PIPPA	TAMMY
POPPY	TATUM
RANDI	TERRY
RICKI	TRIXIE
RORY	VICKI
ROXY	WENDY
SHARI	

B O Y S

ARI	JAMIE
BAILEY	JEREMY
BARNABY	JESSE
BO	JODY
BOONE	KELLY
BRADY	KERRY
BRODY	KIP
CAREY	KIRK
CASEY	KIT
COREY	LEO
DERRY	LUKE
DEVLIN	MAC
FLINT	MAX
HARDY	MICKEY
HOGAN	MITCH
IAN	PATRICK
JAKE	QUINN

REGGIE
RENO
REO
REX
RILEY
RORY
RYAN

TERRY
TOBY
TROY
ZACK
ZANE
ZEBEDY

BLIND DATE NAMES

Obviously it's beyond the power of a name to bestow good looks on your child—that, for better or worse, pretty much depends on genes, luck, and self-esteem. But a name with an attractive aura, like a good telephone voice, can influence other people's expectations and perceptions of someone's looks. Studies back this up: in one bogus beauty competition (see page 124), women of comparable attractiveness were rated with and without name tags. Nameless, the voting was even; when names became a factor, those with plain names were trounced by those with attractive ones.

An attractive name reinforces an attractive image, while an unattractive one contradicts it, can even throw it into question. We know a plain but charming man named Hunter who is wildly successful at getting dates, and admits he wouldn't be so lucky if his name were Melvin. On the other side of the coin is a perfectly nice-looking man named Herb who has, in desperation, resorted to introducing himself by his last name only—which happens to work as an appealing first name as well—and somehow doesn't get around to mentioning his given name until the third or fourth date.

ATTRACTIVE NAMES

Chances are, your sole criterion for a name isn't that it further your daughter's romantic career, but for better or worse, her name can have a lot to do with whether people see her as pretty or plain, foxy or frumpy.

Girls' names with a decidedly attractive image fall into two clear-cut groups: sexy and more delicately pretty. While a glamorous image, for example, will certainly spark your daughter's appeal on the blind-date circuit, you may want to think twice about the ways it will affect the other aspects of her life. Will Desirée make it to the boardroom? Studies say probably not.

The pretty names, however, carry less ambivalence. Some may be a tad soft, a bit flowery, but as a group they're more solidly grounded in the competent adult world.

Names that will arouse a certain anticipation in the opposite sex include:

S E X Y

AMBER	CLEO
APRIL	CRYSTAL
BAMBI	DAWN
BRANDY	DELILAH
BRITTANY	DESIRÉE
CHER	DOMINIQUE
CHRISTIE	FARRAH

GEORGIA
INDIA
JADE
JASMINE
LANA
LAUREN
LILA
LITA
LIZ
LIZA
LOLA
LOLITA
MARGAUX
MARLA

MONIQUE
RAQUEL
RITA
SABRINE
SALOMÉ
SCARLETT
SELENA
STORM
TAMARA
TARA
TAWNY
TEMPEST
VERONIQUE

P R E T T Y

AMANDA
ADRIENNE
ALEXANDRA
AL(L)ISON
ANDREA
ANGELICA
ARIEL
ASHLEY
BRETT
BROOKE
CHLOE
COURTNEY
DEVON
DIANA
EDEN

FRANCESCA
GABRIELLE
HALEY/HAYLEY
HEATHER
HIL(L)ARY
JACQUELINE
JENNIFER
JESSICA
KIMBERLY
LAUREL
LESLIE
LINDSAY/LINDSEY
MELANIE
MELISSA
MIRANDA

MORGAN SABRINA
NATASHA SAMANTHA
OLIVIA TIFFANY
PA(I)GE VANESSA
PAMELA WHITNEY

Call Me Claudette

Whenever a new girl joined up, the first thing she needed was a working name. . . .

To me, certain names have always suggested specific images. A girl named Natalie should have long dark hair. Alexandra is tall and stately, and Ginger is a spunky redhead. I gave the name Melody to a girl named Carol whose voice was so mellifluous it made me think of music. When Wilma joined up, tall, sophisticated, and experienced, I knew immediately that she would be Claudette. . . .

These new names weren't only for the comfort and convenience of the girls, they were equally important to those of us who had to describe the escorts over the phone. When I or one of the assistants was describing a girl to a client, we would have to conjure up an image of her in just two or three phrases. Her name could be a big help in that process.

One day I had the bright idea of buying one

of those *What to Name Your Baby* books as a
way to generate more names. . . . I wrote down
a hundred or so names that I especially liked
and started asking the new girls to make their
selections from that list. . . .

Occasionally I would have to veto one of their
suggestions, because names like Monique,
Noelle, Nicole, and Tiffany made a girl sound
like a hooker. . . .

—Sydney Biddle Barrows with William
Novak, *Mayflower Madam*, Arbor House

Pretty Name, Pretty Woman

If you were shown a picture of a beautiful
woman and told her name was Bertha, would
that actually affect your response to her looks?
The answer is a resounding yes, according to
research conducted by psychologist S. Gray
Garwood at Tulane University.

Garwood staged a mock "beauty contest" on
the Tulane campus, using six pictures of women
who had previously been judged equally attractive. Three of the contestants were given
"desirable" names—Kathy, Jennifer, and
Christine—and three were given "undesirable"
ones—Ethel, Harriet, and Gertrude. (The names'

desirability had been determined by a student survey conducted by Garwood a year earlier.)

The results: Kathy, Jennifer, and Christine garnered 158 votes, compared to only 39 for the unfortunate Ethel, Harriet, and Gertrude. Not only did the men find the attractively named women more attractive; the women voters did, too! The contestants with the "pretty" names received 83 percent of the male and 77 percent of the female vote.

Her mother had given her the name Agnes, believing that a good-looking woman was even more striking when her name was a homely one. Her mother was named Cyrena, and was beautiful to match, but had always imagined her life would have been more interesting . . . if she had been named Enid or Hagar or Maude. And so she named her first daughter Agnes, and when Agnes turned out not to be attractive at all, but puffy and prone to a rash between her eyebrows, her hair a flat and bilious hue, her mother backpedaled and named her second daughter Linnea Elise. . . .

—Lorrie Moore, "Agnes of Iowa"

> Perhaps nothing about a person is more potent, and also more arbitrary, than the person's name.
>
> —Susan Sontag, *Scenes from a New Play,*
> *Alice in Bed,* excerpted in *The New Yorker*

HANDSOME NAMES

Good-looking names for boys can be divided into two categories: nice guys and not-so-nice guys. The nice guys are sensitive and sweet and tend to offer a goodnight kiss at the door; the rogues don't call the next morning, although women usually wish they would.

To facilitate your son's romantic future, consider the following when choosing a name:

HANDSOME NICE GUYS

ADAM	CASS
ADRIAN	COLIN
ALEX	ETHAN
BARNABY	EVAN
BEN	FORREST
CAMERON	FRAZER
CASEY	GABRIEL

GIDEON
GREGORY
GRIFFIN
IAN
JARED
JED
JEREMY
JORDAN
JOSH
JULIAN
JUSTIN
KENYON
LOGAN
MALCOLM

MAX
MILO
NATHANIEL
OLIVER
REED
SAM
SEAN
SIMON
THEO
TOBIAS
TREVOR
TYLER
WADE

H A N D S O M E
R O G U E S

ADDISON
ASH
AUSTIN
BAILEY
BEAU
BRADY
BROCK
CHAD
CLAY
CLINT
CODY
DALLAS
DALTON

DARCY
DAVIS
DENVER
DEVON
DYLAN
FLINT
GAVIN
GRAY
HART
HUNTER
JACKSON
JASPER
JEFFERSON

JESSE	SEBASTIAN
JUDD	SHANE
KEIL	WILEY
LEX	WOLF
LOGAN	WYATT
LUKE	ZACK
QUINN	ZANE
REX	

Overheard by Bob Smith on Macy's main floor, one female shopper to another:

First shopper: He sounds very nice. What's his name?

Second shopper: Bernie . . . [slightly apologetic] . . . but he really doesn't look like a Bernie.

First shopper: So what does he look like?

Second shopper, happily: A Manny.

—Ron Alexander, "Metropolitan Diary,"
The New York Times

Oliver Twist

Oliver . . . goes with my dark, dark hair and kissable ivory teeth, my slim waist, my panache and my linen suit with the ineradicable stain of Pinot Noir. It goes with having an overdraft and knowing one's way around the Prado.

—Julian Barnes, *Talking It Over*

FITTING IN/
STANDING OUT

Picture a nursery school classroom. In the middle of the room is a crowd of ordinary children—those with readily acceptable, blending-in names: the Jennifers and Jasons, the Johns and Janes. Pleasant and convivial, but a little, well, boring. Around the perimeter, standing or playing alone, are the children with names that are unusual, invented, eccentric—the Ravens and Rains, Ivos and Ianthes. Interesting but risky.

Running between the two groups—now blending in with the crowd, now standing out as individuals—are the children with names that are recognizable, yet not epidemic; unusual, but not weird.

Choosing a name that strikes this balance, that will help your child both fit in and stand out, is difficult. Names that do so successfully seem to fall into one of the following groups:

• Less common forms of classic names—Eliza instead of Elizabeth, for instance, or Ned rather than Edward.

- Classic names not widely used today—Philip and Grace, for example.
- Twists on trendy names—Laurel as opposed to Lauren, Alec for Alex.
- Fashionable names at the bottom of the most-popular lists, like Olivia or Duncan.

Names we consider to have found this golden mean include:

G I R L S

ABIGAIL	FRANCESCA
ADRIENNE	GABRIELLA
AMELIA	GEORGIA
ANNABEL	GILLIAN
BIANCA	GRACE
BERNADETTE	HILARY
CAMILLE	HOPE
CASSANDRA	ISABEL
CELIA	JOCELYN
CELESTE	JULIA
CHLOE	JULIET
CLAIRE	JUSTINE
CLAUDIA	KITTY
COLETTE	LACEY
DAISY	LARISSA
DELIA	LAUREL
DINAH	LEILA
ELIZA	LILA
ELLA	LOUISA
EVE	LYDIA

MARA	POLLY
MARGO(T)	ROSE
MARIETTA	ROXANE
MARISA	SABRINA
MARTINE	SELENA
MERCEDES	SIMONE
MEREDITH	STELLA
MIRANDA	SUSANNAH
NATASHA	TAMAR(A)
NELL	TESS
NICOLA	TESSA
NINA	TOBY
NOELLE	VALENTINA
NORA	VERONOICA
OLIVIA	VIOLET
PAULINE	ZARA
PHOEBE	ZOE

B O Y S

ADRIAN	FREDERICK
ALEC	GABRIEL
BARNABY	GORDON
BRYANT	HARRY
CALEB	HENRY
CALVIN	HUNTER
CLAY	JACKSON
COLE	JARED
COLIN	JED
DAMIAN	JONAH
DREW	JUDD
DUNCAN	JULIAN

LEO	PATRICK
LOGAN	PHIL(L)IP
LUCAS	REUBEN
MALCOLM	SEBASTIAN
MARCUS	SETH
MILO	SIMON
NATHANIEL	SPENCER
NED	THEO
NOAH	WADE
OTIS	WILEY/WYLIE
OWEN	ZANE

My own name was problematic. While Jeff and Mary could go to the five-and-dime and find cups and wallets bearing their names—evidence that they belonged to a vast and accepted subset of humanity—Bernard was always out of the question, however much I'd spin the racks and dig in the bins with hope: Andy, Art, Bill, Bobby, Charles.

—Bernard Cooper, *Maps to Anwhere*

ODD NAME OUT?

To you, the name Waldo has worlds more character than William; Mabel is far more appealing than Michelle; Jessamine triumphs over Jessica hands down. But you worry about actually choosing one of these unusual, distinctive, even—yes—eccentric names for your child. Will little Waldo grow up to be a weirdo? Will Mabel be a nursery-school outcast?

No matter how much a champion of the individual you are, indelibly singling out your child with an odd name is a scary thing to do. You don't have to rely completely on guesswork to address your fears: There is a mass of research on how unusual names affect children. Some of the results are comforting. The bad news, however, is really awful:

When a boy named Carroll goes bad, he goes really bad.

Not to say Carls or Christophers don't commit crimes, too; it's just that, all things being equal, Carrolls commit more.

So suggest Drs. Robert C. Nicolay, A. Arthur Harman, and Jesse Hurley, psychologists at Loyola University in Chicago, who, over a five-year period, compared court psychiatric clinic cases of eighty-eight white males with unique names (really unique names like Oder, Lethal, and Vere) with eighty-eight others who had common names. Both groups had similar backgrounds and had committed similar crimes, but those with unusual names had perpetrated four times as many.

"Unique names interfere with normal social interaction and . . . this produces disturbed adjustment," the psychologists conclude. "When a child is given a name that causes embarrassment or confusion as to sex (such as Carroll), is the object of ridicule (Olive), or connotes snobbery (Brentwood), he is going to have to fight for it and this may create emotional problems."

However, we must point out that parents who named their child Lethal probably did not train him for a future in the helping professions.

Berthas and Elmers may get lower grades than Lisas and Michaels, not because they're less intelligent, but because teachers are prejudiced against their names.

Psychologists Herbert Harari and John McDavid asked eighty elementary-school teachers in San Diego to evaluate essays of similar quality on a relatively neutral subject ("What I Did Last Sunday"). The researchers arbitrarily assigned and switched around first names of the fifth- and sixth-grade authors. Sure enough, papers said to be written by children with names like Michael and David received a full grade higher than those of Elmer and Hubert, while Karen and Lisa got a grade and a half higher than Bertha.

Eccentric names breed eccentric kids.

It's a chicken-and-egg question, according to more than one study: Nonconformist parents give their child an unusual name and raise him in an out-of-the-ordinary way. The kid then tries to live up to his name—and his parents' expectations—by becoming distinctive or eccentric.

Before you cross every unusual name off your list of possibilities, consider the opposing evidence:

In real life, the academic performance of Berthas and Elmers, Amandas and Michaels, has more to do with their brains than their names.

Contradicting the "essay study" cited above, psychologists compared the first names of 24,000 students in a midwestern city with their scores on a battery of Science Research Associates (SRA) tests. The heartening conclusion: "[The data] clearly failed to support the hypothesis that unusual or unattractive names are generally or systematically associated with deficits in academic or social functioning.''

Mabels fare better than Waldos, but both may have as good a shot as any kid of doing just fine, thank you.

Girls are more apt than boys to find social acceptance and so avoid psychological problems because of having unusual names, according to research done at the Northern New Jersey Mental Hygiene Clinic by psychologists Albert Ellis and Robert M. Beechley.

Also, girls are more likely than boys to have unusual names, are more likely to find that other people like their names, and are more likely to score high marks on self-acceptance tests, according to Richard L. Zweigenhaft of Guilford College.

After carrying out a study in which he found that of those people listed in both the Social Register and *Who's Who in America*, 70 percent had unusual names and only 23 percent had common names, Zweigenhaft concluded: ''. . . in certain settings (such as the upper class provides) and with certain criteria (such as achievement), having an unusual first name does not have a detrimental effect and might even have a beneficial one.''

If you want to give your child of either sex an unusual name, we suggest you focus on another of Zweigenhaft's conclusions: ''Neither men nor women appear to be at a psychological disadvantage as a result of having an unusual or sexually ambiguous first name.''

So don't give up on Elmer.

The latest research has gotten more sophisticated, taking into account the weight of other variables. Pilot studies by one

Massachusetts psychology professor, for example, indicate that if a person sees a first name he doesn't like, but then is confronted with an attractive person bearing that name, the attractiveness will overcome the negative image of the name, beauty being a more powerful factor. This is confirmed by Gary Leak of the Creighton University Psychology Department, who says, "If you were offered a blind date with an Elmer, you might turn it down. But if you got to know an Elmer in your office, and were exposed to his good looks, sense of humor and other positive qualities, within ten hours, you would forget the name factor."

The Real Reason Movie Stars Don't Live in France

French parents who give their children unusual names like Jade or Cerise are not just taking chances with their children's psyches; they're breaking the law.

An 1803 law drafted under Napoleon, who disliked eccentric names (wonder why?), gives the government final say over parents' choices of names. And if a name is "ridiculous" or "likely to provoke teasing," the court has the power to throw it out and substitute one it deems more suitable.

Judged illegal in recent years have been Prune, Jade, Cerise, Manhattan, and Fleur de Marie. Also rejected recently was, ironically enough, Napoleon—not because of the name itself, but because the child's last name was Lempereur (the emperor). Explained the mayor who turned it down: "We thought it would be just too hard for the little kid to take."

—*The Wall Street Journal*

CLASS STANDING

You want to give your child a name with class, a name that will imbue him or her with an aura of good breeding and refined taste. Even if you're not striving to create an impression of great wealth, at least you don't want to saddle your kid with a name that conjures up trailer parks and greasy spoons.

But class is a sticky issue, and a name's status on the social ladder is constantly shifting. Trying to determine the current class standing of a name can be as difficult as figuring out how much money Donald Trump really has. A few general rules of thumb, however, will provide basic guidance.

- Most names of obscenely rich people (for example, Morgan and Whitney) are downwardly mobile unless you really are a Morgan or a Whitney.
- Also downwardly mobile are names of ridiculously expensive stores or things: Tiffany, Bentley, or Crystal, for instance.

- On the other hand, names used for servants in 1930s movies about obscenely rich people are now upwardly mobile. Bridget, Josephine, Rose, Tillie, Amos, and Patrick have all arrived at the front door.
- Also climbing America's social ladder are eccentric names long favored by British nobility, names like Dinah, Jemima, Sophie, Harry, and Ralph.
- Names more obviously redolent of British nobility, like Amanda, Courtney, and Ashley, are downwardly mobile, however, as are names dripping with Frenchness—Michelle, Danielle, Nicole.
- Upwardly mobile are more homespun ethnic names—Irish, Italian, and Jewish favorites like Margaret, Maria, and Max.
- Also on the way up are plain, quiet names—Jane and John, Nora and Jack—that reflect the current status of conservative living and traditional taste.

These topsy-turvy rules are confusing, yes, but they are based on social principles that can be applied to other things— clothes, furniture, cities—as well as names. Here's how it works: The elite choose names sanctioned by their own social milieu, the middle class imitates the elite, and the working class imitates the middle class. But once a name filters down to the hoi polloi and becomes common, in both senses of the word, the classy image that sparked its popularity is tarnished and it falls out of favor first with the upper class, then with the middle, then with the lower. (Numerous examples of names that quite recently suggested an aura of class, of money and privilege, but are now downwardly mobile will be found in the section on names that are So Far In They're Out.)

The Upwardly Mobile names that are listed below are for

the most part ones that have long been relegated to the lower rungs but whose image is rising, and rapidly. Previously in the mansion's kitchen or out in the fields, these Upwardly Mobile names are now more and more likely to be heard in the nursery.

Upwardly mobile names

G I R L S

AGNES	GEORGIA
ALICE	HARRIET
ANNA	HELEN
ANABEL	HENRIETTA
BEATRICE	ISABEL(LA)
BERNADETTE	IVY
BESS	JEMIMA
BRIDGET	JOSEPHINE
CHARLOTTE	LILY
CHRISTABEL	LOLA
CLAIRE	MADEL(E)INE
CLEMENTINE	MAE/MAY
CLEO	MAGGIE
CLOVER	MAMIE
DAISY	MARGARET
DELILAH	MARIA
DINAH	NATALIE
ELLA	NELLIE
EMMA	NORA
FLORA	OLIVE
FRANCES	PATRICIA

PHOEBE
POLLY
ROSE
SADIE
SALLY
SONIA

SOPHIE
STELLA
TESS
TILLIE
VIOLET

B O Y S

AMOS
BEN(JAMIN)
CALEB
CALVIN
FELIX
FRANCIS
GUS
HARRY
JACK
JASPER

LEO
MACK
MAX
NATHAN
PATRICK
RALPH
SAM(UEL)
SILAS
SIMON
WILL

Among the surprising ups and downs in the histories of names Jane has had her share. At one period she was accustomed to sleep in a grand bedroom and dine at very high tables, but in the nineteenth century she was likely to climb up countless stairs to her menials' attic at night and go to the basement for her meals.

—Ivor Brown, *A Charm of Names*

Names that are too Much, or not Enough, to live up to

Some names are so godlike, so heroic, that they could easily crush a tiny ego before it has a chance to sprout. On the other side of the coin are the names that even a toddler can transcend, names better suited to a parakeet than a person. Beware of giving your child a name that is either too much to live up to, or one he or she will always have to struggle to rise above.

Too much to live up to

ACHILLES	BLISS
AJAX	CAESAR
AMADEUS	CASSANDRA
ANTIGONE	CHASTITY
APHRODITE	CLEOPATRA
ARISTOTLE	DANTE
ATLAS	DESIRÉE

FIDEL
GLORY
GOLIATH
HAMLET
HERCULES
JESUS
JEZEBEL
LAFAYETTE
LANCELOT
LAZARUS
LOTHARIO
LUCRETIA
MAXIMILIAN
MERLIN
MUHAMMED
NAPOLEON
OBEDIENCE
OCTAVIUS

ODYSSEUS
OPHELIA
ORESTES
PLATO
RADCLIFFE
RAMBO
REMBRANDT
RHETT
ROMEO
SALOME
STARR
STORM
TEMPERANCE
TEMPEST
VENUS
WASHINGTON
WELLINGTON
ZOLTAN

Not enough to live up to

BABE
BAMBI
BARBI(E)
BIFF
BIRDY
BITSY
BRANDI/BRANDY
BUBBLES
BUCK

BUD
BUNNY
CANDY
CHERRY
CHIP
CINDY
DEE
DODY
DOLLY

DOM	PEPPER
DUKE	PIP
DUSTY	POPPY
FAWN	RICKY
FLIP	RIP
GOLDIE	SHEP
GYPSY	SHERRY
HY	SISSY
IKE	SKIP
JUNIOR	SONNY
KIT	SUNNY
LES	TAB
LUCKY	TAD
MIDGE	TAFFY
MIMI	TAMMY
MINDY	TAWNY
MISSIE	TIPPI
MUFFIN	TISH
MUFFY	ZERO

I have one regret about my comments . . . about the state of local news on New York television. That is, my flip listing of some reporters' first names. Reporters should be judged by what they know and the job they do, not by their names, especially since Tappy Phillips does a commendable job.

—Jeff Greenfield, letter to the editor,
New York

I always thought of myself as a star . . . I knew I was born to it . . . I think people are named names for certain reasons, and I feel that I was given a special name for a reason. In a way, maybe I wanted to live up to my name.

—Madonna, quoted by Stephen Holder,
The New York Times

If you're considering any of the following names for your child, you just might want to bear in mind that they were recently discovered on a list of most popular names for DOGS!

MAX (2,055 of them in Los Angeles alone!)
BRANDY
SANDY
SAM
SAMANTHA
COCO
MAGGIE
MISSY

The given name is a dead giveaway of our parents' ambition for us—whether to diminish or enhance, ignore us as much as possible or control us forever.

—Fay Weldon, *Darcy's Utopia*

In the dispute over which wields the greater influence, nature or nurture, don't underestimate nomenclature. How many Wilburs find themselves goaded into a lifetime of playground fights over their name? How many Bambis feel compelled to carry their MBAs in their purses to prove they are to be taken seriously?

Is a less-than-queenly first name license for being treated frivolously? Would Hillary be first-name fodder for stand-up comics and sitting congressmen if she were Elizabeth or Anne?

—Patt Morrison in the *Los Angeles Times Magazine*

NO-IMAGE NAMES

What do you think of when you hear the name James? It could be someone as sullenly sexy as James Dean or as smoothly sophisticated as James Bond. In other words, a James, like a John, Jack, or Joseph, can be anything. And, indeed, some names are chosen precisely because they project no specific personality. We asked two mothers we know why they had named their sons Michael, currently the most common boys' name in America. Both gave almost the same reply: With a name shared by so many different types of men comes a certain freedom for the child to be whatever he wants to be. Enough genetic destiny would be imposed on their sons, they felt, without the further constriction of a type-casting name.

But popularity is not enough to guarantee anonymity. Some of today's most-used names—in particular romantically feminine girls' names such as Jessica, Heather, and Amanda—evoke specific expectations.

Names that are truly "no image" tend to be those used

over long periods of time by parents from a cross section of religious, class, and ethnic backgrounds. Most are either short and unadorned or have so many nickname possibilities that there would be one to fit any kind of child.

G I R L S

ANN(E)	JOAN
BARBARA	KATE
CAROL	LEIGH/LEE
ELIZABETH	LYNN
ELLEN	NANCY
JANE	PATRICIA
JEAN	SALLY
JENNY	SUSAN

B O Y S

ALAN	MARK
ANDREW	MATTHEW
CHARLES	MICHAEL
CHRISTOPHER	NICHOLAS
DANIEL	PAUL
DAVID	PETER
EDWARD	RICHARD
JACK	ROBERT
JAMES	STEPHEN
JOHN	THOMAS
JOSEPH	WILLIAM

Mikes, Petes, Sams, Johns, Als, and Bills can grow up to be almost anything they want, while Keiths and Summers have to battle heavy odds to avoid careers in dental caps.

—Russell Baker, "A Name for All Seasons," Sunday Observer, *The New York Times*

[To my father] there were still numbers of names which hung so equally in the balance before him that were absolutely indifferent to him. Jack, Dick and Tom were of this class: These my father called neutral names;—affirming of them . . . that there had been as many knaves and fools at least, as wise and good men, since the world began, who had indifferently borne them. . . . Bob, which was my brother's name, was another of these neutral kinds of Christian names, which operated very little either way; . . . Andrew was something like a negative quality in Algebra with him—'twas worse, he said, than nothing—William stood pretty high—and Nick, he said, was the Devil.

—Laurence Sterne, *Tristram Shandy*

SEX

This section will solve all your sexual problems—at least in the area of naming your child.

Here is where we consider the gender implications of names—from the ultrafeminine to the tomboyish, from the macho to the wimpy—as well as the ever-increasing territory of ambisexual names in between.

When considering names for your baby, you may not have identified sex as the factor that makes one group of names sound appealing to you, another repellent. But most names do have a clear sexual identity, do suggest different degrees of masculinity or femininity. And the fact is that the name you select casts a distinct reflection of how strongly feminine or masculine you want your child to be and appear. If you are suggesting boys' names like Spencer and Miles, and your husband is countering with Rod and Clint, sooner or later he will accuse you of trying to turn your son into a wimp and you will tell him that's better than producing a baby who wears boxing gloves.

We are aware that the sexual reading of names can be subjective. Reactions will be generational (someone picturing the young Dorothy Lamour might wonder how that name ever got into the no-frills category) and individual (you dated a fullback named Dwight in high school and have forever after considered it the most masculine name in the world). You'll be surprised, however, by how many names—because of sound, style or specific connotation—have very distinct sexual profiles.

Your feelings about the sexual image of girls' names may be influenced by your stand on feminist issues. One father we interviewed said that in looking for a name for their daughter, he and his wife applied the following test: Does this sound like a prospective justice of the Supreme Court? As more and more women enter the work force, many parents are seeking an androgynous or no-frills name that will give their daughter an edge with the male competition.

As ambisexual names increase in popularity for girls, however, more parents are looking for traditionally masculine names for boys. While a name like Ashley sounds strong and capable for a girl, it has now lost a certain degree of power as a boy's name. Even the new manly names that reflected the sensitized ideal male image of the seventies are—and we think this may be a sad step backward—declining under the pressures of our brave new world.

One way to approach this section is to consider these issues first and find names that appeal to you and reflect your position. Another option is to draw up a list of names that you like and then use our classifications to make sure their gender implications are the ones you had in mind.

Either method will help you discover the kind of sexual identity you would like your child to project to the world:

the daintiness of a Cicely, the sultriness of a Selena, or the briskness of a Bess; the brute force of a Flint or the sensitivity of a Seth.

I find it entirely appropriate that Sofka should have named her sons after kings and emperors and her daughters as if they were characters in a musical comedy. Thus were their roles designated for them. The boys were to conquer, the girls to flirt. . . . Sofka sees her children's futures as being implicit in their names.*

—Anita Brookner, *Family and Friends*

*Those names were Frederick, Alfred, Mireille (Mimi), and Babette (Betty).

FROM MADONNA TO MERYL

The sexual impact of girls' names seems to break down into four main categories:

Feminissima: The ultrafeminine, often sexy, sometimes fluffy female names, à la Madonna.

Feminine: Female names that suggest a classic sort of femininity.

No-frills: Straightforward names that, while clearly female, have an efficient, no-nonsense air.

Boyish: Names like Meryl that are used for girls but have a boyish or ambisexual image.

Here you'll find specifics on each of these categories, along with lists of names in the four groups.

Now I wonder what would please her,
Charlotte, Julia or Louisa?
Ann and Mary, they're too common;
Joan's too formal for a woman:
Jane's a prettier name beside;
But we had a Jane that died.
They would say, if 'twas Rebecca,
That she was a little Quaker,
Edith's pretty, but that looks
Better in old English books.
Ellen's left off long ago:
Blanche is out of fashion now.
None that I have named as yet
Are so good as Margaret.
Emily is neat and fine.
What do you think of Caroline?

—Charles Lamb

FEMINISSIMA NAMES

If these names were dresses, they would be pale pink, with ruffles and lace and big bows and sprigs of flowers strewn on every available square inch. They are the sweetest of the sweet, the most feminine of the feminine names.

What makes these names Feminissima rather than merely Feminine? Three or more syllables sometimes do it. Soft sounds—s's and f's—can also push a name over the edge from

Feminine to Feminissima. Names that by their meaning suggest ultrafeminine qualities, like Allegra and Lacey, are Feminissima. Very exotic names—especially Latin ones like Raffaela and Gabriella—qualify. And sex-goddess names—from Salomé to Marilyn to Madonna—also connote an exaggerated femininity.

You can hardly give your daughter one of these names without suggesting a little girl with ringlets and rosy cheeks, the kind of child who plays only with dolls (with ringlets and rosy cheeks) and cries if her Mary Janes get scuffed. Her name will make boys want to go on blind dates with her, and other girls see her as a potential threat even before they meet her.

Does that mean that giving your girl a Feminissima name will automatically make her a spineless jellyfish? Quite the opposite. There is something modern about these hyperfeminine names, something liberating about the possibility of an Angelica being chosen vice-president over an Alix. Just as the notion of a female Tyler with long hair and high heels has the appeal of the unexpected, so has that of a Felicia in a business suit or sweat pants.

Feminissima names

ADORA
ADRIANA
ALEXANDRA
ALLEGRA
ALYSSA and variations
ANGELICA
ANGELINA
ANNABELLA

ARABELLA
ARIANA
ARIEL
AURORA
BABETTE
BARBIE
BELINDA
BLOSSOM

CAMILLA
CAROLINA
CASSANDRA
CECILIA
CECILY
CHERIE
CHRISSIE
CHRISTABEL
CICELY
CLARISSA
CRYSTAL
DAWN
DESIRÉE
DOLLY
ELISSA
EMMALINE
EVANGELINE
FAWN
FELICIA
FIFI
FRANCESCA
GABRIELLA
GEORGIANA
GISELLE
HEATHER
HYACINTH
ISABELLA
JOSETTE
JULIANA
LACEY
LANA
LARISSA

LETITIA
LILIANA
LISABETH
LOUELLA
LUCIANA
LUCINDA
MADONNA
MARCELLA
MARIETTA
MARILYN
MARTITIA
MELISSA
MELODY
MERRY
MIRABELLE
MISSIE
MONIQUE
ORIANA
PRISCILLA
RAFFAELA
ROSALINDA
SABINA
SABRINA
SALOMÉ
SAMANTHA
SCARLETT
SELENA
SERENA
SUZETTE
TABITHA
TAFFY
TATIANA

TEMPEST   VANESSA
TIFFANY   VENUS
TRICIA   YVETTE
VALENTINA

FEMININE NAMES

By far the largest group of girls' names is made up of Feminine names: names that are clearly female without being too fussy, sweet without being syrupy, soft without being limp. Many of the most popular girls' names of recent years can be found on this list. Style has favored these decidedly feminine names, along with androgynous names, over either ultrafeminine or no-nonsense female names.

The advantages of a Feminine name are several. Most of these names are easy to understand and easy to like: Your child will hear again and again what a pretty name she has, and that's pleasing. Also, kids like names that are sexually unambiguous; they like labels that clearly identify them as a girl or a boy. And most of these names are familiar, either because of their classic status or because they have been popular in recent times.

What of the future for Feminine names? Some, like Katherine and Elizabeth, are virtually timeless, but many of the names in this group have been so fashionable for several years that they verge on the cliché. If you want to stay away from a name that is already too trendy, be sure to cross-reference any you like here with the So Far In They're Out list in the Style section. One general observation: Many of the hypereuphonic feminine names—Jennifer, Christina, et al.—are on their way out, while more offbeat feminine names, like Annabel, Daisy, Savannah, sound newer and stronger.

Feminine names

ABIGAIL
ADELA
ADELAIDE
ADELINE
ADRIENNE
AILEEN
ALANA/ALANNA
ALEXA
ALEXANDRA
ALEXIS
ALICIA
AL(L)ISON
AMANDA
AMBER
AMELIA
AMY
ANDREA
ANGELA
ANABEL
ANNETTE
ANTONIA
APRIL
ARAMINTA
ARLETTA
AUDRA
AUDREY
BEATRICE
BEATRIX
BECCA
BELLE

BENITA
BERNADETTE
BIANCA
BONNIE
BRIDGET
BRONWYN/
  BRONWEN
CAITLIN
CAMILLE
CANDACE
CARA
CAROLINE
CATHERINE/
  KATHERINE
CECILE
CELESTE
CELIA
CHARMAINE
CHELSEA
CHLOE
CHRISTA
CHRISTIANA
CHRISTINA
CHRISTINE
CLARICE
CLAUDETTE
CLEMENTINE
COLETTE
COLLEEN
CORDELIA

CORNELIA	FERN
CYNTHIA	FIONA
DAISY	FLORA
DANIELLA	FRANCINE
DAPHNE	GABRIELLE
DARLA	GAY
DARLENE	GELSEY
DEANNA	GEORGIA
DEBORAH	GILLIAN
DEIRDRE	GINA
DELIA	GLORIA
DELILAH	GLYNIS
DENISE	GRETCHEN
DIANA	GWENDOLYN
DINAH	HALEY/HAYLEY
DOMINIQUE	HELENA
DONNA	HELENE
DOREEN	HENRIETTA
DORIA	HIL(L)ARY
DOROTHEA	HOLLY
EILEEN	IMOGEN(E)
ELAINE	INGRID
ELENA	IRIS
ELISE	ISABEL
ELIZA	JACQUELINE
ELIZABETH	JANICE
ELOISE	JANINE
EMILY	JASMINE
ESMÉ	JEANETTE
EVA	JENNA
EVELYN	JENNIFER
FEODORA	JESSA

JESSICA	LUCIA
JOANNA	LUCY
JOCELYN	MADEL(E)INE
JULIA	MARA
JULIET	MARCIA/MARSHA
JUSTINE	MARGO
KATHLEEN	MARGUERITE
KEZIA(H)	MARIA
KIMBERLY	MARIEL
KIRSTEN	MARINA
KRISTIN	MARLENE
LANA	MARYA
LARA	MAURA
LAURA	MAUREEN
LAUREL	MEGAN
LAUREN	MELANIE
LEATRICE	MELANTHA
LEILA	MERCEDES
LEONORA	MIA
LIA	MICHELLE
LIANA	MIRANDA
LILA	MOLLY
LILIAN	MONICA
LILY	NANCY
LINDA	NANETTE
LISA	NAOMI
LIZA	NATALIE
LOLA	NESSA
LORETTA	NICOLA
LORNA	NICOLE
LORRAINE	NINA
LOUISA	NOELLE

NOREEN
ODELIA
ODESSA
ODETTE
ODILE
OLIVIA
OPHELIA
PALMA
PALOMA
PAMELA
PANDORA
PANSY
PATRICE
PATRICIA
PAULETTE
PAULINA
PAULINE
PEGEEN
PENELOPE
PETRA
PHILIPPA
PHOEBE
PIA
PILAR
POLLY
QUINTINA/
  QUINTANA
RAMONA
REBECCA
REGINA
RENATA
RENÉE

RHEA
RITA
ROCHELLE
ROSA
ROSALIE
ROSALIND
ROSAMOND
ROSANNA
ROSEMARY
ROWENA
ROXANNE
RUBY
SABINE
SABRA
SANDRA
SAVANNAH
SELENA
SERENA
SHANA
SHANNON
SHARON
SHEENA
SHEILA
SHERRY
SHIRA
SHOSHANA
SIMONE
SONDRA
SONIA
SOPHIA
STELLA
STEPHANIE

SUSANNAH
SUZANNE
SYLVIA
TALIA
TAMAR
TAMARA
TANYA
TARA
TESSA
THEODORA
T(H)ERESA
THOMASINA
TILLIE
TINA
TRISH
VALERIE
VENICE/VENETIA

VERONICA
VICTORIA
VIOLET
VIRGINIA
VIVIAN
WENDY
YASMINE
YOLANDA
YVONNE
ZANDRA
ZARA
ZELIA
ZENA
ZIA
ZOE
ZORAH

NO-FRILLS NAMES

These are the denim skirts of girls' names: clearly not fit for boys, but as straightforward, down to earth, and—sometimes—blunt as you can get while still being female.

One readily apparent difference between these and the more feminine girls' names is that they are shorter: fewer letters and syllables, fewer embellishments. Many end in consonants rather than vowels, which gives them a harder sound. They're almost like generic labeling: Yes, they say, this is a girl, but that's all we're going to tell you.

The No-Frills names here fall into two groups: those with a straightforward sound—direct and to-the-point names like

Jean, Lynn, Ruth—and those with a no-nonsense image: Constance, Gladys, Mildred.

No-frills names

ADA
ADELE
AGATHA
AGNES
ALICE
ANNA
ANN(E)
BARBARA
BERNICE
BERTHA
BESS
BETH
BLANCHE
CARLA
CAROL
CASS
CEIL
CHARLOTTE
CLAIRE
CLAUDIA
CONSTANCE
CORA
CORINNE
DELLA
DIANE
DORA
DORCAS
DORIS
DOROTHY
EDITH
EDNA
ELEANOR
ELLA
ELLEN
EMMA
ENID
ESTELLE
ESTHER
ETHEL
ETTA
EUNICE
EVE
FAITH
FAY
FRANCES
FRIEDA
GAIL
GERALDINE
GLADYS
GRACE
GRETA
GWEN

HANNAH	LENORE
HARRIET	LESLIE
HAZEL	LOIS
HEIDI	LOUISE
HELEN	LUCILLE
HESTER	LYNN
HILDA	MADGE
HONOR	MAE/MAY
HOPE	MAEVE
HORTENSE	MARGARET
IDA	MARIAN
INA	MARIE
INEZ	MARTHA
IRENE	MARY
JANE	MAUD(E)
JANET	MAVIS
JEAN	MAXINE
JILL	MEG
JOAN	MILDRED
JOANNE	MIRIAM
JOSEPHINE	MONA
JOY	NELL
JOYCE	NOLA
JUDITH	NORA
JULIE	NORMA
JUNE	OLIVE
KAREN	PATIENCE
KATE	PAULA
KAY	PAULINE
KIM	PEARL
LEAH	PHYLLIS
LEIGH	PRUDENCE

RACHEL	SYBIL
RHODA	THELMA
ROBERTA	TRUDY
ROSE	VELMA
RUTH	VERA
SADIE	VERNA
SALLY	WANDA
SARA(H)	WILLA
SELMA	WINIFRED
SOPHIE	ZELDA
SUSAN	

BOYISH NAMES

Whitney Houston has one. So do Glenn Close, Meryl Streep, Sean Young, Jodie Foster, Brooke Shields, Daryl Hannah, Mel Harris, Mackenzie Phillips, Michael Learned, Lindsay Wagner, Bo Derek, Drew Barrymore, Quinn Cummings, Barrie Chase, Norris Church, and Christopher Norris. Jamie Lee Curtis has two.

They're Boyish names, and they're increasingly popular for girls. Time was, women hid behind men's names in order to be taken seriously. But where George—as in Eliot or Sand— was once an alias, now it's more likely to be a girl's real name.

There is a long history of appealing heroines with boyish names: from Jo in *Little Women* to Lady Brett in *The Sun Also Rises*. In fact, there are dozens of leading ladies who have played a character with a masculine-sounding name at some point in their careers. Irene Dunne was Ray, for example, and Audrey Hepburn, Reggie; Tuesday Weld, Christian; Bette Davis, Stanley; Olivia DeHavilland, Roy; Janet Leigh, Wally; and Jane Russell, Nancy Sinatra, and Anne Baxter all Mikes.

Sometimes, a name that sounds tired for a boy, like Sydney, becomes fresh and crisp when applied to a girl. Names that can be wimpy for a boy, such as Brooke or Blair, can confer a brisk kind of strength on a girl.

But Boyish names often appeal more to parents than to the child herself. A girl named Kyle may be disturbed by the fact that her male playmate down the block has the same name, and wish she were called something more clearly defined as female, like Jessica. However, most grown-up women with Boyish names say they began to be grateful to their parents for them when they reached the age of about eighteen. At that point, they started to appreciate the sexual ambiguity as well as the sex appeal of having a boyish name.

What follows is a list of Boyish names that are commonly used for girls. If you want to venture further into masculine-sounding names for your daughter, also consult the list of ambisexual names, starting on page 187, and the list of boys' names for girls on pages 189 and 190.

Boyish names

ALI	BILLIE
ALIX/ALEX	BLAIR
ALLY/ALLIE	BO
ASHLEY	BRETT
BARRIE	BROOKE
BERRY	BRYN
BERYL	CAREY

CARLIN
CARLY
CARMEN
CASEY
CHRIS
CODY
COREY
COURTNEY
DALE
DANA
DEVON
DORIAN
EDEN
FLANNERY
GENE
GERMAINE
GERRY
GREER
GWYN
JAMIE
JAN
JESSIE
JO
JODY
JORDAN
KEIL
KELLY
KELSEY
KERRY
KIM
KIT

KYLE
LEE
LESLIE
LINDSAY
MACKENZIE
MALLORY
MEREDITH
MERLE
MERYL
MORGAN
NOEL
PAT
RAE
RANDI/RANDY
RICKI/RICKY
ROBIN
RORY
SACHA/SASHA
SHAWN
SHELBY
SHELL(E)Y
SYDNEY
TERRY
TOBY
TRACY
TRILBY
TYNE
WALLIS
WHITNEY
WYNN

He felt that he could only have relaxed with a woman of a coarser disposition, a dangerous, frankly down-market sort of woman, the sort of woman with whom he need not mind his manners. Whereas Elizabeth—a cool discreet sort of name—treated him with an amiable respect that forced his respect in return.

—Anita Brookner, *Latecomers*

FROM RAMBO
TO SYLVESTER

Boys' names can be divided into four major gender categories. These are:

Macho: Names so hypermasculine they conjure up a frame from *Pumping Iron.*

Manly: The classic male names, used consistently over the centuries, suggesting traditional and clear-cut masculinity.

New manly: Boys' names that have burgeoned in popularity in the postfeminist era. While clearly masculine, these names nonetheless suggest a new, enlightened sort of man.

Wimpy: Sorry, Sylvester, but you're one of the group of male names with a weak image.

In this section, you'll find more details on what these categories mean, as well as lists of names that fall into each one.

Also here is a list of macho men who triumphed over their wimpy names, as well as a section on male names whose sexual image is shifting.

MACHO NAMES

If *Lethal Weapon* was your favorite movie and you're hoping for a little boy who'll strut through the world toting a plastic machine gun and pulling a toy tank, then one of these supermacho names is for you. But remember that even if your little Rod or Bart doesn't look or act like a bull on testosterone, he will always be measured against his name. Girls will giggle, boys will flex their muscles, and nursery-school teachers will wring their hands in anticipation.

Of course, a good many of these names have become jokes: Not many people would name their infant son Attila or Zoltan. But even the more reasonable names carry a lot of hypermasculine baggage. Giving your baby boy one of these macho names is like handing him a football, a hockey stick, and a baseball bat in the nursery and expecting him to play extremely well, or else.

Little Rod or Brock may rebel, the way some particularly well-known guys named Bruce, Arnold, and Sylvester have, but with less desirable consequences. For more on the contrary effect names can have on sexuality, see "Don't Pick a Fight with Bruce," page 183.

Macho names

ANGELO	HUGO
ATLAS	IGOR
AXEL	IVOR
BOONE	JOCK
BRAWLEY	KING
BROCK	KNOX
BRUNO	KNUTE
BRUTUS	MACK
BUBBA	MICK
BURR	OTTO
CLINT	PRIMO
CONAN	RAM
CORD	RAMBO
CURT	RIP
DALLAS	ROCCO
DAX	ROCK
DOLPH	ROCKY
DOMINIC	ROD
DUKE	SAMSON
FLINT	THOR
FORD	VITO
GUS	WOLF
HARLEY	ZOLTAN
HOLT	

MANLY NAMES

The names we call Manly have a Hallmark Father's Day card image: pipe, hunting dogs, golf clubs, the whole caboodle.

They're the men's club of names, the Williams, Fredericks, and Josephs. If, in their proper form, some sound sort of, well, prissy, never fear; they come complete with Manly nicknames: Bill, Fred, Joe.

In terms of style, Manly names are on the upswing. With so many girls' names invading masculine turf—Whitney, Kyle, Alix, et al.—boys' names are retreating to more exclusive ground. And many parents these days want their boys clearly to be boys, names and all.

Boys tend to fare well with these sturdy, classic names. No one ever gets teased for being called David, for instance, and no little Frank is ever mistaken for a girl on the basis of his name. The price you pay for this safety is that your son may not feel unique: There are relatively few classic boys' names and the selection is not all that inspired.

At the same time, the long craze for less traditional boys' names—the Jamies and Coreys, the Joshuas and Jasons of the last twenty years—freshens the sound of stalwarts like Henry and Fred. We may be moving back to the days when "every Tom, Dick, and Harry" was more than just a figure of speech.

Manly names

AL(L)AN/ALLEN	CHARLES
ALBERT	DANIEL
ALFRED	DAVID
ANDREW	DONALD
ANTHONY	DOUGLAS
ARTHUR	EARL
BERT/BURT	EDWARD
CARL	FRANK

FREDERICK
GEORGE
GERALD
GORDON
HAROLD
HARRY
HARVEY
HENRY
HOWARD
HUGH
IVAN
JACK
JAMES
JOHN
JOSEPH
KENNETH
LAWRENCE
LEO
LEONARD
LEWIS/LOUIS
MARK
MARTIN
MICHAEL
NEAL/NEIL
NED
NORMAN

PATRICK
PAUL
PETER
PHIL(L)IP
PRESTON
RALPH
RAYMOND
REX
RICHARD
ROBERT
ROGER
RONALD
ROY
RUSSELL
SAMUEL
STANLEY
STEPHEN
STUART/STEWART
THEODORE
THOMAS
VICTOR
VINCENT
WALTER
WARREN
WILLIAM

NEW MANLY NAMES

The last decade has seen the emergence of a new breed of names: names that bespeak a transformed masculine ideal—

sensitized, enlightened, liberated from the manacles of ma-chismo. Names for guys who shop and cook and diaper their babies. Guys who cry.

Some of these New Manly names have already worn out their welcome, while others remain in vogue. Although a certain percentage, like Jonathan and Joshua, have tradi-tional roots, for the most part these names have been in wide use only since the publication of *The Feminine Mystique*. This is not to suggest that they are feminine names. Most are unmistakably male, but neither are they muscle-bound, far right, or radical.

This group of names is for little boys who may still prefer to play with trucks and build with blocks, but who probably also have at least one anatomically correct doll on their shelves.

It reflects the imagination of the first generation of parents not to rely on the inert pool of traditional male names for their sons. In the mid-sixties, names like Eric, Scott, and yes, Jason started appearing on the list of the top fifty names for boys; by 1982, Jason was number five and a flock of other Newly Manly names from Justin to Joshua to Jonathan had unseated such old standbys as Arthur, Frederick, and Peter.

One reason for the wild rise in popularity of these New Manly names is that it became unfashionable to name a boy after his father or any other family patriarch. Patriarchy itself was unfashionable. Each child was seen as an individual, to be given a fresh and creative start in life.

While many of these names are still popular, as a group they are not as stylish as they were even a few years ago. Most of the boys' names on the So Far In They're Out list can be found here. Exceptions are many of the surname names, as well as newcomers like Rex, Clay, and Duncan that buck the Tom, Dick, and Harry tradition but haven't been as overused as the Jason and Joshua group.

In addition, many of the new place names and surname-names would fit into this category.

New manly names

AARON	BEVAN
ABEL	BLAINE
ABNER	BLAKE
ADAM	BRADLEY
AIDAN	BRADY
ALEC	BRANDON
ALEX	BRENDAN
ALEXANDER	BRETT
AMOS	BRODY
ANGUS	BRYANT
ANSON	CALE
ARI	CALEB
ARLO	CALVIN
ASHER	CAMERON
AUSTIN	CAMPBELL
AVERY	CAREY
BAILEY	CARSON
BARNABY	CARTER
BARTHOLOMEW	CARVER
BEAU/BO	CASE
BEN	CASEY
BENEDICT	CHRISTIAN
BENJAMIN	CHRISTOPHER

CLANCY	EL(L)IOT(T)
CLAY	ELISHA
CLEMENT	ELLIS
CODY	EMANUEL
COLIN	EMMETT
COOPER	EPHRAIM
COREY	ERIC
CURTIS	ETHAN
DALE	EVAN
DALLAS	EVERETT
DALTON	EZRA
DAMIEN/DAMIAN	FABIAN
DANE	FORREST
DARCY	FOSTER
DASHIELL	FRASER
DAVIS ✓	GABRIEL
DENVER	GARRETT
DEREK	GIDEON
DEVLIN	GRAHAM
DEVON ✓	GRAY/GREY
DIRK	GREGORY
DONOVAN	GRIFFIN
DRAKE	HALE
DREW	HUBBELL
DUNCAN	HUNTER
DUSTIN	IAN
DYLAN	ISAAC
EBEN	ISAIAH
ELI	JACKSON ✓
ELIA	JACOB
ELIAS	JAKE
ELIJAH	JAMIE

JARED	LANE
JARRETT	LEMUEL
JARVIS	LEVI
JASON	LIAM
JASPER	LINCOLN
JED	LINUS
JEDIDIAH	LIONEL
JEFFREY	LOGAN
JEREMIAH	LOREN
JEREMIAS	LORNE
JEREMY	LUCAS
JESSE	LUCIAN✓
JODY	LUCIUS
JON	LUKE
JONAH	MACKENZIE✓
JONAS	MALACHI/
JONATHAN	MALACHY
JORDAN	MALCOLM
JOSH	MARC
JOSHUA	MARCO
JOSIAH	MARCUS
JUD(D)	MASON
JUDE	MATTHEW
JULIAN	MATTHIAS
JUSTIN	MAX
KAI	MAXFIELD
KEIL	MAXWELL
KEIR	MICAH
KENT	MILO
KIRK	MORGAN
KYLE	MOSES
LANDON	NATHAN

NATHANIEL
NED
NICHOLAS
NOAH
NOEL
NOLAN
OLIVER ✓
OMAR
OTIS
OWEN
QUENTIN
QUINN
RAPHAEL
REDMOND
REED
RENO
REO
REUBEN
RILEY ✓
ROBINSON
ROLLO
RORY
ROSS
ROWAN
RUFUS
RUPERT
RYAN
SAM
SAUL
SAWYER
SEAN/SHAWN

SEBASTIAN
SETH
SHANE
SILAS
SIMON ✓
SOLOMON
SPENCER
TAYLOR
THADDEUS
THEO
TIMOTHY
TOBIAH
TOBIAS
TRACY
TRAVIS
TREVOR
TRISTAN
TYLER ✓
WALKER
WEBB
WILEY/WYLIE ✓
WILL
WYATT
WYNN
YALE
ZACHARIAH/S
ZACHARY
ZACK/ZAK
ZANE
ZED
ZEKE

WIMPY NAMES

No matter how sensitive you want your son to be, you surely don't want to brand him as a wimp. You don't want to give him a name that will get him picked last for every team, shunned in every game of spin the bottle, turned down for every blind date.

Unfair as it may seem, the Selwyns and Percys and Egberts of this world tend to meet one of two terrible fates. Either they knuckle under to their names, and *become* Selwyns or Percys or Egberts; or they bust their gonads proving that, despite the wimpy label, they're really Rods or Brunos or Rambos.

We have been conservative in devising this list. We have avoided borderline wimpy names, and concentrated on the hard (soft?) core group. What relegates a name to terminal wimpdom?

Once-ambisexual names now used almost exclusively for girls qualify: Lynn or Courtney, for example. A feminine sound, like the sibilant Percival or Sylvester, can push a name into the wimp category. And any name ending in "-bert" (Hubert, Egbert, Wilbert) or "-ville" (Melville, Orville) or "-wyn/vin" (Selwyn, Melvin) almost automatically triggers a wimp response in the modern ear.

This brings up a salient point for any of you out there with decidedly nonwimpy uncles or fathers named Bernard or Melvin. Perceptions of wimpiness tend to change over generations. As Russell Baker points out (see page 186), Jason was once one of the biggest wimp names going. And a name that seems perfectly substantial for a fifty-year-old man can suddenly go limp when applied to a newborn baby of today.

Obviously, this list is intended more as a warning than a guidepost. If you're determined to go ahead with one of these names, maybe you should be prepared to spend your old age introducing Delmore as "My son, the butterfly collector" or "My son, the mercenary guerrilla." Tough choice.

Wimpy names

AINSLEY	DABNEY
ALGERNON	DELMORE
ALOYSIUS	DEWEY
ALVIN	DURWOOD
AMBERT	DWIGHT
ARNOLD	EGBERT
BENTLEY	ELBERT
BERNARD	ELLSWORTH
BERTRAM	ELMER
BLAIR	ELROY
BROOKE	EUGENE
BROOKS	FARLEY
BRUCE	FERDINAND
BURTON	GALE
CARLTON	GAYLORD
CARROLL	GOMER
CECIL	HARLAN
CEDRIC	HARMON
CHARLTON	HERBERT
CLARENCE	HERMAN
CONWAY	HUBERT
COURTNEY	HYMAN
CYRIL	IRA

IRVING
IRWIN
JULIUS
KERWIN
LANCE
LEON
LESLIE
LESTER
LYNDON
LYNN
MANFRED
MARION
MARLON
MARMADUKE
MARVIN
MAURICE
MAYNARD
MELVILLE
MELVIN
MERLE
MERLIN
MERTON
MERVYN
MILTON
MURRAY

MYRON
NORBERT
ORVILLE
OSBERT
OSWALD
PERCIVAL
REGINALD
RODNEY
SANFORD
SELWYN
SEYMOUR
SHELDON
SHERMAN
SHERWOOD
SYLVESTER
THURMAN
VANCE
VERNON
VIRGIL
WENDELL
WESLEY
WILBERT
WILBUR
WILFRED

Don't Pick a Fight with Bruce

A wimpy name does not necessarily a wimpy boy make. In fact, the world is full of Bruces, Arnolds, and Sylvesters we wouldn't want to meet in a dark alley. Maybe these guys became supermacho in reaction to their anemic names, or maybe they would have overdeveloped biceps even if their names were Brawley or Flint. Here, a list of famous tough guys with anything but tough names.

ARNOLD Schwarzenegger
BROOKS Robinson
BRUCE Jenner
BRUCE Lee
BRUCE Springsteen
BRUCE Weitz
CARLTON Fisk
CARROLL O'Connor
CECIL Cooper
CHARLTON Heston
CLARENCE Clemons
DWIGHT Gooden
ELROY Hirsch
ELVIS Presley
ERNEST Borgnine
ERNEST Hemingway
EVANDER Holyfield
FRAN Tarkenton
GALE Sayers
GAYLORD Perry
JULIUS Erving
HARMON Killebrew
HERSCHEL Walker
HUMPHREY Bogart
LEON Spinks
LYNDON Johnson
LYNN Swann
MARION Motley
MARLON Brando
MARVIN Hagler
MEL Gibson
MERLE Haggard
MERLIN Olsen

OREL Herscheiser	SYLVESTER Stallone
REGGIE Jackson	THURMAN Munson

What Jason Was

When I was a child, only the most sadistic parents named their children Jason. . . . Like Percy and Horace, Jasons existed only to be beaten in the schoolyard by classmates named Spike and Butch.

—Russell Baker, "A Name for All Seasons,"
Sunday Observer, *The New York Times*

BEACH BOYS

In the late fifties and early sixties, no names were cooler than Gary, Glenn, and Greg. They were the personification of surfer machismo. Now, however, these Beach Boy names have lost their muscle. They are too old to be new men, too young to be manly, too soft to be macho, and too firm to be truly wimpy. This group of masculine nomads includes:

BRAD	CHAD
BRIAN	CRAIG

DARREN   KEITH
DARRYL   KEVIN
DEAN   RICK
DENNIS   SCOTT
DUANE/DWAYNE TODD
GARY   TROY
GLENN   WAYNE
GREG

At five, Marlon had an angelic face and a pugnacious nature, developed as a defense against neighborhood bullies who taunted him about his fancy-sounding name.

> —The Star, excerpted from Brando:
> A Biography in Photographs,
> by Christopher Nickens

AMBISEXUAL NAMES

The trend over the past twenty years has increasingly been to bestow ambisexual names upon girls rather than boys. And once a name moves from the male province into the female, there's usually no going back.

There have been a number of transsexual shifts in the history of nomenclature. Alice, Anne, Crystal, Emma, Esmé, Evelyn, Florence, Jocelyn, Kimberly, Lucy, and Maud all were originally male names. Christian was a feminine name in the Middle Ages, as was Douglas in the seventeenth century and Clarence in the eighteenth. A king of East Anglia in the seventh century was named Anna.

In the sixties, it was more usual to find a boy with an ambisexual name than it is now. The big trend in that consciousness-raising time was toward cute nicknames that sounded just as right for boys as for girls: Jody, Toby, Jamie. This continued in the seventies with ambisexual nicknames that were short for more sexually distinct proper names. There were plenty of Chrises, Nickys, and Alexes around, but on their birth certificates they were Christopher or Christine, Nicholas or Nicole, Alexander or Alexandra.

More recently we've moved back to ambisexual proper names without nicknames, but, as detailed in the Androgynous Executive list in the What's Hot section, these are used more and more for girls rather than boys. While a carriage bearing an Alexis, Blair, or Jordan may still hold a boy, it's more likely that the blanket in it will be pink and the baby will be female.

In the vanguard of style, parents are even considering traditionally masculine names for their daughters. One couple we know—a television producer and a theatrical lawyer—said that if their child was a girl, they would name her George.

We've arranged the following list of Ambisexual names from those that are at the moment used almost exclusively for girls to those used primarily for boys. When a name had variant spellings for boys and girls, we've included both, but with nickname names like Ricky and Terry, we've listed only the ambi y ending.

This list can be a help in determining the current gender standing of a name. But, be warned: We predict that by the turn of the next century many of the names in the 50 percent range will have moved into the feminine dominion, and that names like Jordan and Perry and Daryl may well be considered about as appropriate for a boy as, say, Sue.

90 percent feminine

ALLIE/ALLY
ANDREA

CAROL (f);
CARROLL (m)

CHRISTIE/CHRISTY
CLAIRE (f);
  CLARE (f,m)
COURTNEY
EVELYN
GAIL (f); GALE (f,m)
HA(Y)LEY
HIL(L)ARY
JOYCE
KAY

LACEY
LAURIE
LESLIE/LESLEY
LYNN
MARIAN/MARION
PA(I)GE
PATSY
SHANNON
TRACY

75 percent feminine

ALEXIS
ALI
ANGEL
ASHLEY
BLAIR
BROOKE
BRYN
DANA
JAN
KELLY
KELSEY
KERRY
KIM

KIT
LAUREN (f);
  LOREN (f,m)
LINDSAY/LINDSEY
MALLORY
MEREDITH
MERRILL
ROBIN
SACHA/SASHA
SHELL(E)Y
STACY
WHITNEY

50/50

ALEX
BO
BRETT
CAREY
CASEY
CASS
CHRIS
DAKOTA
DALE
DARCY
DEVON
DORIAN
FRANCES (f);
 FRANCIS (m)
GERRY (f,m);
 JERRY (f,m)
HOLLIS
JAMIE
JEAN (f); GENE (f,m)
JESS(I)E

JODY
JORDAN
KAI
LANE
LEE (f,m);
 LEIGH (f)
MACKENZIE
MORGAN
NICKY
PAT
PAYTON
RICKY
SHAWN (f,m);
 SEAN (m)
STORM
TAYLOR
TERRY
TOBY
WALLIS (f,m);
 WALLACE (m)

75 percent male

BAILEY
BLAKE
CAMERON
COREY
DARIN/DARREN
DAR(R)YL

DREW
DYLAN
ELLERY
EMLYN
EVAN
KEIL

KIRBY
KYLE
MICKEY
NEVADA
NOEL (m,f);
    NOELLE (f)
NORRIS
PALMER
PARKER
PERRY
PORTER
QUINN
RANDY
RAY (m,f);
    RAE (f)

REED
REGAN
RORY
SAM
SCHUYLER
SHELBY
SIDNEY (m)
SIERRA
SLOAN
SYDNEY (m,f)
TYLER
VALENTINE
WALKER
WYNN
YAEL

90 percent masculine

ADDISON
AIDAN
AL(L)AN/ALLEN (m);
    ALLYN (m,f)
BROWN
CHRISTOPHER
CLAUDE
DALLAS

GARY
GEORGE
GLENN
MEL
MICHAEL
SETH
SHANE
ZANE

No Boys Named Maria

In 1932, the Supreme Court of Czechoslovakia ruled that Maria would no longer be allowed as a name for male children. The tribunal decided that a given name must clearly denote an individual's sex.

"By the time Jamie goes to college, it's probably going to cost about $29,000 a year. Either I'd better make some smart decisions or else she'd better learn to play football."

—Citibank TV commercial

TRADITION

"**H**akeem?" "Here." "Liam?" "Here." "Sarita?" "Here." Attendance-taking time at any self-respecting preschool these days will tell you that tradition as an influence on naming is back with a vengeance.

You, like many parents, may be looking into your own familial history—canvassing the names of grandparents, great-aunts, and uncles—to come up with a name for your child that reflects your cultural heritage. You may be considering a family surname for your baby's middle or even first name, whether your child is a boy or a girl. And if a suitable name can't be plucked from your own family tree, you may find yourself wandering into other orchards in search of a seasoned name, a name with substance.

To give you a perspective on the past, we offer here a history of this century's naming trends, the fashions and fads that typified each decade. Also here is a guide to nicknames: the rise and fall in popularity of a range of abbreviated forms, including some no longer used versions—Daisy for Margaret, for example, or Hobbin for Robert—you may find worth consideration.

You may want to incorporate tradition in your child's name by choosing one that reflects your ethnic heritage. Let's say you're German, and you'd like to explore options beyond the obvious Otto and Fritz. In one section here you'll learn that Andreas, Axel, and Arno, among others, would all be authentically German choices, even though you may have believed otherwise. Another chapter will give you some exotic names from other cultural backgrounds, from Hebrew to Italian to Polish. And if you're looking for a name to reflect black heritage, included here are lists of Arabic and African names.

If your hope is to come up with a name that connects to the religious traditions of your family, you may want to consult the list of unexpected saints' names—and take this book to the baptism to convince the priest there really is a Saint Benno. Also here is a guide to Jewish naming traditions, including examples of how the first-initial practice and secular trends have combined to bring naming patterns full circle.

Our focus on tradition narrows in the chapter called Family Ties. Are you and your spouse wrestling over name choices? Here's why, plus tips to help you come to a compatible decision. If you're thinking of making your son a junior, you'll find the pros and cons here. Also here is a guide to sibling names—for first-time parents, too! And finally, we offer a primer on living with your ultimate choice of name.

Here, then, to Tradition, the fourth important factor in choosing the right name for your child.

AMERICAN NOMENCLATURE

TRADITION IN PROGRESS

There are two currents of tradition in American names.

One is really an English tradition, names brought over by the Pilgrims and handed down from generation to generation, from century to century. Mary, Ann, Catherine, and Elizabeth; John, James, Charles, Joseph, Robert, William, and Edward were as well used here in 1750 as they were in 1900 and as they are today, but are no more uniquely American than, say, an *Oxford Dictionary*.

A naming tradition America could call its own didn't really blossom until 1920. By that time, when our parents' parents bobbed their hair and shaved their mustaches, put in a phone, and searched for modern baby names, there were places to look: at the marquee of the new movie theatre down the block, to the voices on the radio now dominating the living room, or at the neighbors who just arrived from County Cork.

American tradition is one part history and three parts experimentation, fashion, and progress—with a strong dash of folly. To get a true picture, you have to consider chili dogs along with apple pie, Groundhog Day as well as the Fourth of July, Mickey along with Michael.

Here, a look at the naming tradition we've just begun to create.

The 64 Percent Solution

It has been estimated that in fourteenth-century England 64 percent of all male children were given one of the following five names:

HENRY
JOHN
ROBERT
WILLIAM
RICHARD

Today, by contrast, roughly the same proportion of boys receive names ranked in the top fifty.

The 1920s and 1930s:
Freckles, France, and Hollywood

The hottest trend in the 1920s and early 1930s was freckle-faced names for girls and boys, Our Gang comedy names that came complete with button noses, big ears, and overbites. A lot of these were nicknames for perennial favorites—Billy or Willie for William, for example, or Margie, Maggie, and Peggy for Margaret—but others were proper names you just don't hear much anymore:

G I R L S

BETSY	PATSY
BINNIE	PEGGY
DOLLY	PENNY
GWEN	POLLY
KATHLEEN	SALLY
KITTY	TRUDY
MARY ANN	WINNIE

B O Y S

BARNEY	FRANKLIN
CALVIN	HAL
CHESTER	HOMER
CLEM	MICKEY
DEXTER	NED
ELMER	WILBUR
EUGENE	WILLIS

At the same time, several names, often those popularized by stars, were new arrivals on the best-seller list. For girls: Alice,

Barbara, Betty, Jean, Marion, Myrna, Patricia, Shirley, and Virginia; for boys, Arthur, Clarence, Donald, Harry, Henry, Richard, and Thomas.

Other female fads for the period included names of the months (April, May, and June); names ending in the letter *s* (Phyllis, Frances, Doris, Lois, Iris); and names ending in *-een* or *-ine*—Irish ones like Eileen, Maureen, Pegeen, Noreen, Kathleen, and Colleen, or more Gallic specimens like Jacqueline, Maxine, Arlene, Nadine, Pauline, and Marlene, which followed in the wake of such earlier favorites as Irene, Geraldine, and Josephine. Even more fashionably French were Annette, Claudette, Paulette, Georgette, Jeanette, and Nanette, not to mention Rochelle, Estelle, and Isabel.

Diamond-Studded Names

What were the most glittery names of 1927? Or at least what did the copywriters of the Sears, Roebuck catalog of that year think would appear as such to their constituency when they decided to give girls' names to the various models of "Genuine Brilliant Diamond Rings"?

They were:

ABBIE	BEULAH
ALICE	CLARICE
ANGELA	ELAINE
ANNA MAY	ELEANOR
ANNETTE	FLORENCE
BETTY JANE	GENEVIEVE

HONORA	MARILYN
INEZ	MILDRED
IRENE	MINERVA
JANET	PAULINE
KATHRYN	RUTH
LORRAINE MAY	VIOLA
LYDIA	

The 1930s and 1940s: Hi Mom! Hi Dad! I'm home!

During the mid-thirties through the forties, names like Dorothy, Anne, Shirley, Ruth, George, Frank, Edward, and Clarence fell off the top ten, to be replaced by Carol, Judith, Joan, Linda, Ronald, and David. Other new names were moving in as well—"sophisticated" names for kids whose parents envisioned them triumphing over the Depression and growing up to use cigarette holders, wear glamorous evening clothes, and live in Hollywood-inspired mansions. Television was still in its infancy, so no one could foresee that these would become the sitcom mom and dad names of the next generation:

G I R L S

ANITA	CYNTHIA
ARLENE	DEBORAH
AUDREY	DIANE
BEVERLY	ELAINE
BRENDA	ELLEN

GAIL	NATALIE
JANET	PAMELA
JOANNE	RENÉE
LORRAINE	ROBERTA
LYNN	SANDRA
MARILYN	SHEILA
MARJORIE	SUSAN
NANCY	

B O Y S

AL(L)AN/ALLEN	MITCHELL
BARRY	NEIL/NEAL
CHRISTOPHER	NORMAN
EL(L)IOT	PAUL
EUGENE	PETER
GERALD	PHIL(L)IP
HAROLD	ROGER
HARVEY	ROY
HOWARD	RUSSELL
IRA	STANLEY
JOEL	STEPHEN
LAWRENCE	VINCENT
MARTIN	WALTER
MICHAEL	WARREN

The 1950s: Ranch houses and barbeques

The postwar baby boom moving into the fifties spawned a whole new generation of cuter, younger, glossier names, names for kids who would play with Tiny Tears dolls and watch Captain Kangaroo, oblivious to the hard times just past. These names reflected a collective lust for a new way of life, the good life in the suburbs. Linda jumped from number ten to number one in popularity and Karen appeared out of nowhere to take the tenth spot. Michael, a Biblical name that had been out of favor for over a hundred years, catapulted to number two. Other newly popular names in the fifties, many of which remained in vogue through the Kennedy administration, were:

G I R L S

AMY	JANICE
CHARLENE	JULIE
CHERYL	LISA
CHRISTINE	MICHELLE
DARLENE	ROBIN
DENISE	SHARON
DONNA	TERRY
HEIDI	TINA
HOLLY	WENDY

B O Y S

ANDREW	ERIC
ANTHONY	GARY
BRIAN	GREGORY
BRUCE	JEFFREY
CRAIG	KENNETH
DEAN	KEVIN
DENNIS	LEE
DOUGLAS	MARK

MATTHEW   TERRY
PATRICK   TIMOTHY
SCOTT   TODD

The 1960s: Do your own thing

In the sixties and early seventies, as men grew their hair to their shoulders and women abandoned their bras, Karens and Craigs gave way to Caryns and Chastitys, Kellys and Clouds. In deference to the new credo of "do your own thing," new names were invented, familiar forms of old names became perfectly acceptable, and the spelling of traditional names became a contest of creativity. The ultimate trendy name of the sexually liberated sixties and early seventies was actually a relaxed nickname name, preferably ambi-gender. We saw a lot of the following:

CANDY   MANDY
CARRIE/CAREY   MARCY
CASEY   MARNIE
CINDY   MINDY
COREY   RICKI/RICKY
JAMIE   SHARI
JESSIE/JESSE   SHELL(E)Y
JODY   SHERRY
JONI/JON   STACY
KELLY   TAMMY
KERRY   TAWNY
KIM   TRACY
LORI

Even more revolutionary were such invented hippie names as:

AMERICA	PEACE
ASIA	PHOENIX
BREEZE	RAIN
CHE	RAINBOW
CHINA	REBEL
CLOUD	RIVER
DAKOTA	SEASON
DUNE	SENECA
ECHO	SEQUOIAH
FOREST	SIERRA
FREE	SKY
GYPSY	SPRING
HARMONY	STAR
LEAF	STARSHINE
LIBERTY	SUMMER
LIGHT	SUNSHINE
LOVE	TRUE
MORNING	WELCOME
OCEAN	WILLOW

The Names, They Are A-Changing

Now that lovebeads and elephant bells are nostalgia items, many of the flower children's children are trading in their hippie names for more mainstream ones. Zowie Bowie, for instance, son of David Bowie, now calls himself Joey. Free, born to David Carradine and Barbara Hershey when she was calling herself Bar-

bara Seagull, has changed his name to Tom.
And Susan St. James, who named her first two
children Harmony and Sunshine, called her sons
born in the eighties Charlie and William.

The 1970s: Ahead to the past

The mid-seventies saw the beginnings of a reawakening of
patriotism, but this tentative romance was with a pre-
Watergate, pre-Vietnam, pre-Bomb, pre-Depression, pre-
Industrial Revolution America—way back to the Old West.
Fifty years after the birth of a uniquely American naming
tradition, we finally summoned the confidence to delve back
into our country's own past, launching a nation of little ur-
ban cowboys and their pioneer-women sisters named:

G I R L S

AMY	JESSIE
ANNIE	KATIE
BECKY	MAGGIE
JENNY	MOLLY

B O Y S

ETHAN	JOSH
JASON	LUKE
JED	SHANE
JESSE	ZANE

Also, Biblical names like Aaron, Adam, Benjamin, Jacob, Jonathan, Rachel, Rebecca, Sarah, and Samuel were born again, even if the parents choosing them weren't.

Those who couldn't or didn't want to reach back to the frontier or the Bible for their roots looked to their own or other people's ethnic backgrounds for inspiration (see Roots, page 244). Names derived from the Irish or French became particularly popular, even for parents who weren't Irish or French. Thus were born thousands of Brians, Dylans, Erins, Kellys, Kevins, Megans, Ryans, Seans, Shannons, and Taras. For girls, the French twist was the rage, with names such as Danielle, Michelle (given a big boost by the Beatles song), and Nicole.

Other little girls were liberated from female stereotypes with names previously reserved for effete upper-class gentlemen: Ashley, Blake, Brooke, Courtney, Kimberly, Lindsay, and Whitney. Similar in tone, although they were always girls' names, are Hayley (as in Mills) and Tiffany (yes: a Charlie's Angel).

At the opposite end of the scale is a group of girls' names as purely feminine as a lavender sachet. These are the wildly popular Victorian valentine names, which include Alexandra, Alyssa (in all its variant spellings), Amanda, Jennifer, Jessica, Samantha, Melissa, Vanessa, and Victoria. Their male counterparts are Alexander, Brett, Justin, and Nicholas.

The 1980s: Upward Mobility

The eighties were the decade of Gekko-greed, double-digit inflation, Reagonomics, Abscam, Yuppies, Cabbage Patch Kids, Charles and Diana, and Calvins. It was also the decade of the baby boomlet and of the first generation of mothers who were more likely to work outside the home than to take care of the kids. Feminism made concrete, upward mobility, and a strong emphasis on image all conspired to influence naming trends of the era.

In 1980, Jennifer still reigned supreme. The top ten girls' names of that year form a transitional bridge between the soul-searching seventies and the neoconservative Reagan-Bush era. They were:

1.	Jennifer	6.	Michelle
2.	Amy	7.	Heather
3.	Melissa	8.	Amanda
4.	Kimberly	9.	Erin
5.	Sarah	10.	Lisa

By the middle of the decade, most of these names vanished from the top-ten hits. At decade's end, only the two most classic—Sarah and Amanda—remained.

Other classic names, which evidenced the good taste and traditional values prized in the decade, were restored, with legions of eighties' babies named Katherine, Elizabeth, Emily, William, Daniel, Andrew, and Christopher. Working moms and feminist dads sought naming equality in the eighties, too, giving both daughters and sons upwardly mobile androgynous names such as Jordan and Morgan and Alex and Blake. Ashley, one such name that emerged for children of both sexes during the seventies, enjoyed a meteoric rise for girls throughout the eighties, now topping out at number one.

While the eighties and many of its values ended with a crash, several of its naming trends survive, with a decidedly nineties twist. The past decade's veneer of old money has been replaced by a more solid emphasis on genuine family histories, with names that honor real ancestors rather than those that conjure phony WASP pedigrees. Ethnic names and surnames, as well as place names and non-glitzy family names, are more fashionable than the slick choices of the eighties.

The passing of the eighties marks our official goodbye to Jennifer and Jason, now fallen far from favor and supplanted by such newcomers as Cameron and Chelsea, such rejuvenated classics as Caroline and Charles.

THE HUNDRED-YEAR CYCLE

When was the last time that names like Alexander, Benjamin, Amanda, and Gregory were in vogue? A startling number of the names that sound fresh and appealing to us today were favored by the new parents of a hundred years ago. Appearing in the top-fifty lists a century ago were:

G I R L S

ANNIE	LAURA
CARRIE	LILLIE
CHARLOTTE	LUCY
ELIZABETH	REBECCA
EMILY	SARA(H)
JENNIE	SOPHIA
KATHERINE	

B O Y S

ALEXANDER	HENRY
ANDREW	JACOB
BENJAMIN	JAMES
CHARLES	JOHN
DAVID	SAMUEL
EDWARD	WILLIAM
HARRY	

Other names that didn't make the top fifty but were in fashion a hundred years ago, and are back in style now, include:

G I R L S

AMANDA	LOUISE
CHRISTINA	MADELINE
CLAIRE	MAGGIE
DAISY	OLIVIA
JULIA	POLLY
LEAH	RACHEL

B O Y S

AARON	JOSHUA
ADAM	LUKE
ANTHONY	MAX
BEN	NATHAN
ERIC	NOAH
GREGORY	PATRICK
JESSE	SETH
JONAH	TIMOTHY
JONATHAN	

CATHERINE, KATHARINE, AND KATHRYNNE

You've always loved the name Catherine. But you want your Catherine to be unique; different from all others in the world, so you decide to spell it Kathrynne.

You see the first signs of trouble while still in the hospital, where you are asked to spell the name eleven times. This is followed by similar requests from friends, parents, in-laws, aunts, and cousins, who nevertheless send cards and little pink panda bears addressed to Katharine, Katherine, Kathryn, Kathrinne, and Kathy Lynn.

Creative naming was one of the least felicitous minirevolutions to take place during the Age of Aquarius, when suddenly there was a nonaggressive army of Alicias, Alishas, Alysias, Alisas, Alyssas, Elissas, Elyssas, Ilysas, and Ilyssas peacefully coexisting in the park with Arons, Jaysens, Kristoffers, and Jimis.

While the use of unconventional spellings is no longer epidemic, the practice continues. Recent aberrations noted on birth announcements have included Kassie, Kacie, Kaitlin, Crystine, Holli, Malissa, Megean, Ryann, Jayme, and Jaimie.

Many of these children will grow up surrounded by people who think they don't know how to spell their own names, or that their parents (this means you) were simply ignorant. Poor Megean will have to spend countless hours explaining whether her name rhymes with Pegeen, Regan, or leg in, and many more hours correcting all the people who spell her name wrong by spelling it right.

A different issue arises when a name has bona fide variant spellings, each of which is widely used and accepted. Once again, Catherine is a case in point: the C spelling is originally French and commonly used in Britain; Katherine is the most common form in the United States and Canada; Katharine is derived from the name's Roman version and also well used here; and Kathryn is a spelling used since the turn of the century and popularized in the 1940s by the actress Kathryn (b. Zelma) Grayson.

Other names with more than one well-accepted spelling include Ann/Anne, Sara/Sarah, Alison/Allison, Stuart/Stewart, Teresa/Theresa, Alan/Allan/Allen, Geoffrey/Jeffrey, Lee/Leigh, Philip/Phillip, and Stephen/Steven.

While all these names are pronounced the same whatever the spelling, which form you choose seems to alter the name in subtle ways. Katherine, for instance, seems somewhat hipper than Catherine, which has a more feminine and gently old-fashioned connotation. Ann seems more no-nonsense than Anne, Leigh more delicate than Lee, Geoffrey more buttoned-up than Jeffrey.

When there is more than one correct spelling of a name, let your own feelings on the image each conjures up be your guide. Catherine, Katherine, Katharine, and Kathryn are all perfectly correct choices, and all a far sight better than (please don't) Kathrynne.

THE HILLARY ERA

When Barbara Bush became first lady, there were no front-page commentaries written on the subject of her given name. Yet even before Bill Clinton was inaugurated, there was a page one discourse on the name Hillary in *The Wall Street Journal*. Granted, it was written by a reporter named Hilary (one 'l'), who had a vested interest in the name, but for the American public at large, the name seemed to carry a disproportionate significance, with the consequence that Mrs. Clinton has become almost as much a single-name phenomenon as Madonna, with magazine article after article addressing "The Hillary Question," "The Hillary Complex," "The Hillarys," etc.

Just as the names of Barbara, and her predecessor Nancy, were representative of their eras, Hilary (the preferred spelling) is a name for the nineties. The *WSJ* quoted a spokesman for Mrs. Clinton as saying the first lady was given her name in 1947 because her parents thought it sounded exotic and unusual. No longer really exotic, it is nonetheless still distinctive, strong, powerful, even corporate. It has the three-syllable form so popular right now, without the ultra-femininity of a Melissa or Tiffany. In fact, it is an androgynous name, sometimes—especially in England—still given to boys.

The name Hilary derives from the Latin *hilarius*, which means—you guessed it—"cheerful." The name of a fourth-century saint, it was used as a male name in Great Britain until the seventeenth century, then was revived as a girl's name in the 1890s. As of this writing, it is still not a particularly popular name in the United States, but there *were* eighty-one of them born in Pennsylvania in 1991 (coincidentally the same as the number of Barbaras), and early 1992 figures show the figure to be climbing. It will be interesting to see what effect a dynamic personality like Mrs. Clinton will have on baby-naming in the next few years.

One thing we're already certain of is that no name could be more "in" than the one the Clintons bestowed on their daughter, inspired by the lyric of a Judy Collins song they admired. Chelsea—a trendy place name—is already number seventeen on the list, and our educated guess is that it has nowhere to go but up.

A GRAND OLD NAME

For three centuries, from the days when Mary was dressed in sober gowns of Puritan gray, to the days when she wore a bustle, to the days when she bobbed her hair, her name was always the most popular. The Greek and New Testament version of the Hebrew Miriam, Mary was considered too holy for mortal use until the twelfth century; by the sixteenth, it had become the most frequently used girl's name, a position it held until 1950.

That year, Linda made headline news by toppling Mary from the number-one spot. Mary continued on a downward slide, dropping to number fifteen in 1970 and thirty-four in 1983. Even the current resurgence in classic names has not boosted Mary back into favor.

The problem may be that Mary has become more of an icon than a name. Besides its association with the Blessed Virgin, it has a persistently ethnic ring and a fade-into-the-woodwork quality. Three hundred years of popularity have turned it into a generic term.

The name Mary remains fascinating, however, because of all the ways it has been used and the variations it has spawned. Some Catholic parents, for instance, use it as a token first name, followed by a sprightlier middle name by which their child is known. All four female members of the Fisher quintuplets, born in 1963, were named Mary: Mary Ann, Mary Magdalene, Mary Catherine, and Mary Margaret. And two of Robert and Ethel Kennedy's four daughters are named Mary—Mary Courtney and Mary Kerry—but called only by their middle names. The idea is that, since a Catholic child must carry a saint's name, Mary is sanctified enough to cover all bases, including a "heathen" middle name.

More often, when Mary is linked with another name, both are used. This "Mary-plus" trend reached its height in the 1940s and continued into the fifties, with variations ranging from the sedate Mary Ann and Mary Frances to the hep Mary Sue and Mary Jo to the oh-so-cute twins named Mary Pride and, yes, Mary Joy.

If the Mary-plus fad has (thankfully) gone the way of poodle skirts, derivations of the name Mary have become somewhat more common in this country. Those used here include:

MARA	MARINA
MARIA	MARIS
MARIAH	MARIS(S)A
MARIAN/MARION	MARLA
MARIAN(N)A	MARLENE
MARIANNE	MARLO
MARIBEL	MARYA
MARIE	MAURA
MARIEL	MAUREEN
MARIETTA	MAY
MARIETTE	MERRY
MARILEE	MIA
MARILYN	MOLLY
MARIN	

The name Mary has no fewer foreign variations, which include the Irish Maire and Moira, the French Manette, the British Marigold, and—back to the source—the Hebrew Miriam.

VARIATIONS ON A THEME

When we were growing up, you weren't cool if you didn't have a nickname. Patti, Judy, Billy, and Bobby would rather have traded in their Beatle boots than be known to the world as Patricia, Judith, William, and Robert. The epitome of keen was to have a name that nobody could formalize when they were mad at you, a name that was a nickname: Jamie, Jody, Ricki.

When President Carter signed in as Jimmy in 1976, many people felt buoyed by the symbolism. He was a common man, leader of a nation of Toms and Daves, Kathys and Debbies. But by the eighties, the general sentiment was that a Jimmy wasn't up to such a serious job: We elected a Ronald and then a George, and readopted the formal names on our own birth certificates, becoming Davids and Deborahs and Richards ourselves.

So, too, in the eighties did we favor unabbreviated forms for our children. Little Elizabeths were more likely to lisp through all four syllables of their name than to call themselves Beth or Betsy or Lizzie or any of the other nicknames so popular when we were kids.

Today, we've become a little more flexible, like Bill Clinton, who is always Bill except on formal documents, when he reverts to William Jefferson Clinton. We're turning away both from nickname-names that can't be formalized—the Jamies and Jodys so popular in the sixties and seventies—as well as from the formal appellations in vogue in the neoconservative eighties, giving our children a choice. Today's kids are being named Joseph and called Joe, named William and called Will, named Elizabeth and called Libby.

The problem with these convertible names is how to keep people from using the wrong nickname. How do you, for instance, name your child Edward, call him Ned, but discourage others from descending to Eddie? And what if you like the formal version of a name—Susannah, say—but detest Sue or Susie?

Some parents resign themselves to enforcing their nickname of choice throughout life, to saying (often through clenched teeth), "It's not Eddie. It's Ned. WE HATE THE NAME EDDIE!!!" Others sidestep the nickname issue entirely by choosing a name with no common diminutive: Claire, for example, or Ethan.

The practice of nicknaming can be traced back to the ancient Egyptians, and became widely used in medieval England, where there were so few Christian names in general usage that it was not unusual for two children in a family to have the same name. The only way to distinguish the two James was for one to be called Jamey, the other Jem.

Many proper names that have remained in common use since that time have accumulated a procession of nicknames that reflect changing styles. Today's Katherine, for instance, is most often called Kate, while Kathy was the favored form in the fifties and Kay harkens back to the thirties. Some once-popular nicknames—Tetty for Elizabeth, for instance, and Hob for Robert—have died out, while others have been so well used that they are now considered names in their own right. Nancy, for instance, was once a nickname for Anne, as was Sally for Sarah, Lisa for Elizabeth, and Harry for Henry.

Here, names with a wide variety of nicknames, including some fresh choices you may not have considered:

B A R B A R A

BAB	BABS
BABBY	BARB
BABE	BARBIE
BABETTE	BOBBIE

C A T H E R I N E / K A T H E R I N E

CASS	KATY
CASSIE	KATYA
CAT	KAY
CATHY/KATHY	KIT
KATE	KITTY
KATIE	

E L I Z A B E T H

BESS	LIBBY
BESSIE	LILIBET
BET	LISA
BETH	LIZA
BETSY	LIZBETH
BETTE	LIZETTE
BETTINA	LIZZIE
BETTY	LIZZY
ELISA	TETSY
ELIZA	TETTY

M A R G A R E T

DAISY
GRETA
MADGE
MAG
MAGGIE
MAISIE
MARGE
MARGIE
MARGO

MARGOT
MARGY
MEG
MEGAN
MEGGY
PEG
PEGEEN
PEGGY

M A R Y

MAL
MALLY
MAME
MAMIE
MARE
MAY

MIMI
MINNIE
MITZI
MOLL
MOLLY
POLLY

P A T R I C I A

PAT
PATSY
PATTI
PATTY

TISH
TRICIA
TRISH

R I C H A R D

DICK	RICHIE
HICK	RICK
HITCH	RICKY
RICH	

R O B E R T

BERT	HOB
BOB	NOB
BOBBY	ROB
DOB	ROBBIE
DOBBIN	ROBIN

The Pete Pan Syndrome

A good case against calling your child by any
kind of nickname can be found in the results of
a study headed by Von Leirer, a psychologist
at Human Cognition Research in Stanford, California. Students were asked to judge six fictitious
people—two with formal names (like Peter),
two with familiar ones (Pete), and two with
"adolescent" nicknames (Petey). The Peters
were rated as more conscientious, more emo-
tionally stable, and more cultivated than the
Petes and Peteys.

Everyone else has a nickname. Hilary is Hil, Stephanie is Steph, Alex is Al, Joanne is Jo, Tricia is Trish, Sandy is San. Pat and Liz, who cannot be contracted any further, have become Pet and Lizard. Only Ronette has been accorded the dignity of her full, improbable name.

—Margaret Atwood, *Wilderness Tales*

ROYAL NAMES

What's more traditional, in our English-speaking world, than a royal name, one backed by centuries of use for the kings and queens, princes and princesses of Great Britain? The surprise is how many of these time-honored royal names go beyond the expected Elizabeth and Henry, Charles and Anne, offering a wide range of choices for the modern parent in search of a name that's both adventurous and well-established. Although we've culled out the early, now-obsolete Saxon names like Ethelbald and Elfweard, what follows is a complete list of British royal names for the past milennium:

Royal Names

F E M A L E

ADELA	EDITH
ADELAIDE	ELEANOR
ADELIZA	ELIZABETH
AGATHA	EMMA
AGNES	EUGENIE
ALBERTA	EUSTACIA
ALESIA	FRANCES
ALEXANDRA	GABRIELLA
ALICE	GERTRUDE
AMELIA	GRACE
AMICE	HELEN
ANNE	HELENA
ARABELLA	HENRIETTA
ARBELLA	IDA
AUGUSTA	ISABEL
AVELINE	ISABELLA
BEATRICE	JACQUETTA
BERENICE	JANE
BLANCHE	JOAN
BRIDGET	JUDITH
CAROLINE	JULIA
CATHERINE	JULIANA
CECILIA	LAURA
CECILY	LOUISA
CHARLOTTE	LOUISE
CONSTANCE	LUCY
DAVINA	MARGARET
DOROTHEA	MARINA

MARTHA
MARY
MATILDA
MURIEL
OLIVIA
PHILIPPA
ROSE

SARAH
SIBYLLA
SOPHIA
URSULA
VICTORIA
WILHELMINA
ZARA

M A L E

ADOLPHUS
ALBERT
ALFRED
ANDREW
ANTHONY
ANTONY
ARCHIBALD
ARTHUR
AUGUSTUS
CHARLES
DAVID
DUNCAN
EDGAR
EDMUND
EDWARD
EGBERT
EUSTACE
FRANCIS
FREDERICK
GEOFFREY
GEORGE
GILBERT

GODWIN
GUY
HAMELIN
HAROLD
HARRY
HENRY
HUGH
HUMPHREY
JAMES
JASPER
JOHN
LIONEL
LOUIS
MATTHEW
NICHOLAS
OCTAVIUS
OTTO
PATRICK
PAUL
PETER
PHILIP
REGINALD

RICHARD
ROBERT
ROGER
SIMON
STEPHEN

THEOBALD
THOMAS
VICTOR
WILLIAM

SCOTTISH ROYALS

Until the first years of the seventeenth century, Scotland had its own royal family and its own set of royal names. We haven't included Macbeth (yes, he was real), but we are intrigued by these Scottish royal choices:

Scottish royal names

F E M A L E

AFRIKA
AMABEL
ANNABELLA
BETHOC
CHRISTIAN
CHRISTINA
DONADA
EUPHEMIA

FINNUALA
HELEN
JANET
JEAN
MARGARET
MARJORIE
MATILDA

M A L E

ALAN
ALEXANDER

ANDREW
ANGUS

ARCHIBALD
COLIN
CONSTANTINE
DAVID
DOLFIN
DONALD
DUFF
DUNCAN
DUNGAL
FINLAY

HAROLD
HUGH
KENNETH
MALCOLM
MALISE
NEIL
PATRICK
ROBERT
WALTER

THE KOSHER CURVE

In general, except for the comparatively few people who are using Hebrew names for their children, there is no such thing as a "Jewish" first name anymore. The days when Molly Goldberg sticking her head out of her Bronx tenement window and calling down to her son Sammy meant immediate ethnic identification are long gone. These days, Sam's last name could just as readily be Gallagher and Mrs. Goldberg's son could be named Sean.

When today's Samuels and Benjamins are namesakes of Jewish great-grandpas, the phenomenon can be explained by an interesting theory concerning the cycles that occur in the naming patterns of immigrant families. According to the theory, first-generation immigrants typically renounce any clue to their ethnicity and so choose names for their children prevalent in general society. It is not until the third generation, or even later, that there is enough psychological distance for people to reembrace their ethnic heritage and incorporate it into their lives.

This is evidenced by the naming history of Jewish families in this country. The children of early immigrants turned to the most Anglo-Saxon sounding names they could find, lighting in particular upon aristocratic British surname-names like Stanley and Sheldon, Morton, Milton, and Melvin.

The following chart tracks some representative American Jewish given names from the turn of the century to the present.

ABE · ARTHUR · ALAN · ADAM · AARON
ANNIE · ANN · ANITA · AMY · ANNIE
BEN · BERNARD · BARRY · BRIAN · BEN
CLARA · CLAIRE · CAROL · CARRIE · CLAIRE
DORA · DOROTHY · DIANE · DEBBIE · DAKOTA
FANNY · FRAN · FRANCES · FRANCESCA · FANNY
HANNAH · HELEN · HARRIET · HAYLEY · HANNAH
HARRY · HENRY · HARRIS · HARRISON · HENRY
ISAAC · IRVING · IRA · IAN · ISAAC
JAKE · JACK · JEROME · JAY · JAKE
JENNY · JEAN · JANICE · JENNIFER · JENNA
LILY · LILIAN · LINDA · LORI · LILY
MAX · MARVIN · MITCHELL · MICHAEL · MAX
MOLLY · MARIAN · MARSHA · MARCY · MOLLY
NELLIE · NORMA · NANCY · NICOLE · NELL
RACHEL · RHODA · ROCHELLE · RICKI · RACHEL
ROSE · RUTH · RENÉE · RANDI · ROSIE
SADIE · SYLVIA · SUSAN · STACY · SADIE
SAM · SHELDON · STEVEN · SCOTT · SAM
SARAH · SELMA · SHEILA · SHELLY · SARAH
SOPHIE · SHIRLEY · SHARON · SHERRY · SOPHIE

Popular belief to the contrary, naming a Jewish child after a deceased relative is not mandated by any religious law or biblical test. Rather, the practice springs from a Jewish folk-lore belief that a person's name is his soul. In the Ashkenazic (Jews whose families originated in middle Europe) tradition, naming a child after a living relative could rob the relative of part of his soul and thus shorten his life. Today, even many nonreligious Jews carry a vestigial resistance toward naming a child after a living relative or friend.

This custom, however, is not practiced by Sephardic Jews (whose origins are in Southern Europe, North Africa, and the Middle East), who will name a child after a living relative. Traditionally, paternal grandparents are honored first, followed by maternal grandparents and then aunts and uncles. Infrequently, the child of a Sephardic family will even be named after a parent.

In both cultures, a baby usually isn't given the exact name of the person he is honoring, but a secular name with the same first letter as that person's Jewish or Hebrew name. The reason is not superstition, but simply that many parents don't like the ancestral name.

Double naming—giving a child both a mainstream and a religious name—began in the Middle Ages when the use of names taken from local languages had become so rampant that rabbis decreed that each Jewish boy be given a Hebrew (or otherwise sanctified) name at the time of his circumcision. Having two names soon became the custom for all Jewish babies; a child would have a sacred name, by which he would be called up to read to Torah, as well as a secular name for nonreligious purposes. First-generation American Jews would take their Hebrew names, say Avraham, and anglicize them to any English name beginning with the same initial, from the obvious Abraham to the more assimilated-sounding Arthur or Arnold.

The revival of the Hebrew language in Israel has prompted many American Jewish families to adopt traditional Hebrew names for their babies. Among the most popular are:

HEBREW NAMES

G I R L S

ADIRA	LIORA/LEORA
ALIZA(H)	MICAELA
ARIEL(LE)	MICHAL
ASHIRA	MORIA(H)
AVIGAIL	OFRA
AVIVA(H)	ORA(H)
AZIZA	PUA(H)
CHAVA	SARAI
DALYA/DALIA	SHIRA(H)
DENORA	TALIA
DINAH	TAMAR
ELAMA	TOVA(H)
GALIA	TZURI(Y)A
GAVRILLA	VARDINA
JOELLA	YAEL
KELILA	YAF(F)A
KIRYA	YONA(H)

B O Y S

ADIN	AMON/AMNON
AHARON	ARI
AITAN	ASA

AVI	JONAH
AVNER	LAEL
AVRAM	LEVI
AZRIEL	MALACHI
BOAZ	MATAN
CHAIM	NOAM
DOV	ORI
EITAN/EYTAN	RAM
ELAD	SHAUL
ELI	TAL
ELISHA	URI
EMANUEL	URIAH
EPHRAIM	YAAKOV
ERAN	YITZHAR
GAVRIEL	YOAV
GIDEON	YOEL
GILAD	ZACHARIAH
ISAIAH	ZIV
JAEL	ZOHAR

THE GOOD BOOK OF NAMES

The Bible, particularly the Old Testament, has always been a prime source of names for children in America, dating back to the Hephzibahs and Zedekiahs of Colonial times. But, even with this timeless source, there are trends and fashions. In our day, Sarah, Benjamin, Jonathan and Joshua, Rachel and Rebecca, Adam and Aaron, popular for the past twenty-five years, have just about peaked, while Hannah and Leah are rapidly advancing.

Some fresher-sounding choices might include:

FEMALE

ABIGAIL	BETHIA
ADAH	DEBORAH/
ADINA	DEVORAH
AIAH	DEENA
BATSHEVA/	DELILAH
BATHSHEBA	DINAH

ELISHEVA
ESTHER
EVE
HADASSAH
JAEL
JEMIMA/YEMIMA
KETURAH
KEZIA(H)
LILITH
MARA
MICHAL

MIRIAM
NAOMI
ORPAH
SHIFRA
TAMAR
THIRZA
YEDIDA
ZILLAH
ZIPPORAH
ZORAH (place name)

M A L E

ABEL
ABIEL
ABNER
ABRAHAM
ABSALOM
ADLAI
AMOS/AMOZ
ASA
ASHER
BOAZ
CALEB
ELEAZAR
ELI
ELIJAH
ELISHA
EMANUEL
ENOCH
EPHRAIM

ESAU
EZEKIEL
EZRA
GABRIEL
GERSHOM, GERSON
GIDEON
HIRAM
ISAAC
ISIAH
JABEZ
JARED
JAVAN
JEDEDIAH
JEREMIAH
JETHRO
JOAB
JOEL/YOEL
JONAH

JOSIAH
JUDAH
KENAN
LABAN
LEVI
MALACHI
MICAH
MOSES
NATHANIEL
NOAH
OBADIAH
OMAR
OZNI
PHINEAS

RAPHAEL
REUBEN
SAMSON
SAUL
SETH
SIMEON
SIMON
SOLOMON
TOBIAS
URIAH/URI
YOAV
ZACHARIAH
ZEBADIAH

FABIAN, PATRON SAINT OF ROCK AND ROLL, AND OTHER UNUSUAL, LIVELY, AND SURPRISING SAINTS' NAMES

If, because of tradition or religion, you want to give your child a saint's name, you don't have to settle for obvious choices like Anne, Cecelia, Anthony, or Joseph. Yes, there really is a Saint Fabian, as well as Saints Chad, Benno, Phoebe, Susanna, and Colette. What follows is a selective list of unexpected saints' names.

F E M A L E

ADELA

ADELAIDE

AGATHA

ALBINA

ANASTASIA

ANGELA

ANGELINA

ANTONIA

APOLLONIA

AQUILINA

ARIADNE

AUDREY

AURIA

AVA

BEATRICE

BEATRIX

BIBIANA

BRIDGET/BRIGID

CANDIDA
CHARITY
CHRISTINA
CLARE
CLAUDIA
CLEOPATRA
CLOTILDA
COLETTE
COLUMBA
CRISPINA
DARIA
DELPHINA
DIANA
DOROTHY
EBBA
EDITH
EMILY
EMMA
EUGENIA
EULALIA
EVA
FABIOLA
FAITH
FELICITY
FLORA
FRANCA
GEMMA
GENEVIEVE
HEDDA
HYACINTH
IDA
ISABEL

JANE
JOANNA
JOAQUINA
JULIA
JULIANA
JUSTINA
LELIA
LEWINA
LOUISA
LUCRETIA
LUCY
LYDIA
MADELEINE
MARCELLA
MARINA
MARTINA
MATILDA
MAURA
MELANIA
MICHELINA
NATALIA
ODILIA
OLIVE
PAULA
PETRONILLA
PHOEBE
PRISCILLA
REGINA
RITA
ROSALIA
SABINA
SALOME

SANCHIA
SERAPHINA
SILVA
SUSANNA
TATIANA
THEA

THEODORA
THEODOSIA
VERENA
WINIFRED
ZENOBIA
ZITA

M A L E

AARON
ABEL
ABRAHAM
ADAM
ADOLF
ADRIAN
AIDAN
ALBERT
ALEXANDER
ALEXIS
AMBROSE
AMIAS
ANSELM
ARNOLD
ARTEMAS
AUBREY
AUSTIN
BARDO
BARNABAS
BARTHOLOMEW
BASIL
BENEDICT
BENJAMIN

BENNO
BERTRAND
BLANE
BORIS
BRENDAN
BRICE
BRUNO
CASSIAN
CHAD
CLEMENT
CLETUS
CLOUD
COLMAN
CONAN
CONRAD
CORNELIUS
CRISPIN
CYPRIAN
CYRIL
DAMIAN
DANIEL
DECLAN
DIEGO

DONALD	ISIDORE
DUNSTAN	ISRAEL
EDMUND	JASON
EDWIN	JOACHIM
ELIAS	JONAH
EPHRAEM	JORDAN
ERASMUS	JULIAN
ERIC	JULIUS
ERNEST	JUSTIN
EUGENE	KEVIN
EUSTACE	KIERAN
FABIAN	KILIAN
FELIX	LAMBERT
FERDINAND	LEANDER
FERGUS	LEO
FINNIAN	LEONARD
FLAVIAN	LINUS
FLORIAN	LLOYD
GERARD	LUCIAN
GILBERT	LUCIUS
GILES	MALACHY
GODFREY	MARIUS
GREGORY	MAXIMILIAN
GUNTHER	MEL
GUY	MILO
HENRY	MOSES
HERBERT	NARCISSUS
HILARY	NOEL
HUBERT	NORBERT
HUGH	OLIVER
HUMBERT	OSWALD
ISAAC	OTTO

OWEN
PIRAN
QUENTIN
RALPH
RAYMOND
REMI
ROCCO (Italian
version of
Saint Roch)
RODERIC
RUFUS
RUPERT
SAMSON

SEBASTIAN
SILAS
SIMEON
SIMON
SYLVESTER
THEODORE
TITUS
VIRGIL
WILFRED
WOLFGANG
YVES
ZACHARY
ZENO

Parents should choose suitable names for their children, avoiding such as are obscene, ridiculous or impious. It is advisable that the name of a saint or of some other person distinguished for holiness be chosen, for this will be of a spiritual advantage to the child and an edification to others.

—*Codex Iuris Cononici*, Rome, 1917

"It's Mel," Gibson explains, "not Melvin. Mel is actually an old Irish name. They've got a cathedral in Ireland called St. Mel's. I don't

really know how Mel got to be a saint. There
was probably some nepotism involved, because
Mel was a cousin of Saint Patrick."

—Mel Gibson, quoted in *Premiere* magazine

ITALIAN BATTALION

Traditional Italian-American families adhere to a strict naming procedure brought over from Italy, in which everybody is
named after somebody else. Here's how it works:

First son is named after father's father
First daughter.............. father's mother
Second son .... mother's father
Second daughter.......... mother's mother
Subsequent sons .... father's brothers, in order of age.
                         If you run out, mother's
                         brothers.
Subsequent daughters ... father's sisters, in order of age.
                         When you finish with them,
                         mother's sisters.

This practice radically simplifies the naming decision, especially since, until this generation, most Italian families were
so large it was tough to exhaust the entire store of possibilities. It also leads to lots of children with the same names.
To prevent too much overlap, variations are permissible and
often used, especially for girls' names. Grandma Rosemarie,
for instance, may have namesakes called Rose, Maria,

Annemarie, Rosanne, and Mary. Grandpa Anthony, whose name cannot be varied as easily, is likely to spawn a veritable legion of Anthonys.

Assimilation, intermarriage, and the trend to smaller families are combining to endanger this sort of name inbreeding. While it's sad to lose such a finely tuned tradition, there is an up side: When you call your child at a family reunion, fifty people don't come running.

ROOTS

Shortly after he took the heavyweight championship from
Sonny Liston in 1964, Cassius Clay announced to the world
that he had joined the Nation of Islam and was discarding
his "slave name" in favor of Cassius X, soon switched to
Muhammad Ali. By renaming himself, Ali was in the vanguard of a movement that was to burgeon in the late sixties,
when many blacks adopted the Muslim religion and took
on—for themselves and for their children—Islamic names. In
1971, basketball star Lew Alcindor—not a Black Muslim but
a member of the orthodox Hanafei sect—changed his name
to Kareem Abdul-Jabbar. Other black athletes, entertainers,
and public figures followed suit.

At the same time, some people were looking back to their
African heritage in search of an ethnically valid name, a
trend heavily reinforced by the widely seen television mini-
series, *Roots*, in 1977. Playwright LeRoi Jones became Imamu
Amiri Baraka and soon it was not uncommon to hear tribal
names like Ashanti and Akuba in the playground. Still other

parents chose to honor heroes of black American history. Playwright and actor Douglas Turner Ward, for instance, abandoned his given birth name of Roosevelt in favor of a combination of the names of abolitionist Frederick Douglass and revolutionary slave Nat Turner.

Black parents who wish to pay homage to their past have a vast menu of unusual names from which to choose. Following is a selection of both Arabic and African names.

ARABIC NAMES

Muslim names usually derive from those of the Prophet Muhammad's descendants or immediate family. There are five hundred variations of the name Muhammad itself; taken together they become the most common boy's name in the world. Other popular Arabic names, such as Karim and Kamil, represent the ninety-nine qualities of God listed in the Koran.

G I R L S

ABIDA	AYASHA
ABIR	AZA
ADARA	BARAKAH
ADIVA	BATHSIRA
AISHA	CALA
AKILAH	FATIMA
ALAIA	FATUNAH
ALIYA	HABIBAH
AMINA	HATIMA
ARA	HINDA

JAMILA	NUR
JENA	OMA
JINAN	RAJA
KARIDA	RIDA
KARIMA	RIHANA
LAILA	RIMA
LEILA	SALIMA
LOELIA	SHAHAR
MAJIDAH	TABINA
MOUNA	YASMEEN
NIMA	ZADA
NUMA	ZAHIRA

B O Y S

ABDUL	HASSAN
ADBDULLAH	HUSAIN
AFIF	IBRAHIM
AHMAD/AHMED	JAFAR
AKBAR	JAMIL
AKIL	JUMAH
ALI	KADAR
ALLAH	KAMALI
AMEER	KAMIL
AZIM	KARIM
DAWUD	KASIM
FARIO	MALIK
HAKEEM	MEHMET
HAMAL	MUHAMMAD
HAMID	NURI
HANIF	OMAR
HASHIM	RAFI

RAHMAN   YASIR
SHARIF   YAZID
TAHIR   ZAKI

If you have a hundred sons, name them all
Muhammad.

—Muslim proverb

I used to open my act with a joke: "Hi, I'm
Arsenio. A very unique name for a black man.
In Greek, it means 'Leroy.' "

—Arsenio Hall in *The Hollywood Reporter*

AFRICAN NAMES

G I R L S

ABA   ADIA
ABBEBA   AFRIKA
ABEBI   AIDA
ABINA/ABENA   AINA
ADESINA   AINKA

AISHA	LAYLA
AKIBA	LULLA
AKUBA	LULU
ALUNA	MAIZAH
AMINAH	MANDISA
AMMA	MASIKA
APRILI	MIATA
AZIZA	MONIFA
BARAKA	MULU
CAMISHA	MWAKA
CHIKU	NAEEMA
CHIRIGA	NAFULA
DALILA	NASSOMA
DAYO	NAYO
FAIZAH	NEEMA
FAYOLA	NNENIA
GAMILA	NOBANZI
HABIBAH	NYALA
HALIMA	NYASHA
HANA	OBA
HASINA	PANYA
IMENA	RAMLA
JAHA	RASHIDA
JAMILA	SABAH
JANI	SALMA
JINA	SANURA
KAMBO	SHANI
KANIKA	SHARIFA
KASSINDA	SHIBA
KATURA	SUMA
KAYA	TABIA
LATEEFAH	TALIBAH

TARANA	ZAHARA
TISA	ZALIKA
YABA	ZENA
YAHIMBA	ZINARA
YAMINAH	ZUWENA

B O Y S

ABASI	DAMISO
ABEEKU	DULANI
ADIKA	EBO
ADOM	GYASI
AGU	HAJI
AJANI	HASANI
AKIL	IDI
AKONO	JABARI
ANKOMA	JAFARI
ASHANTI	JAJA
ASHON	JELANI
ATSU	JIMIYO
AYANA	JOJO
AYUBU	JUMA
AZIBO	KAJOMBO
AZIZI	KALUNGA
BASHIRI	KAMUZU
BELLO	KANYE
BEM	KIJANA
BENO	KITO
BOMANI	KOJO
CHUMA	KWAMI
COUJOE	KWAMIN
DAKARAI	KWASI

LADO	PAKI
LIU	RAJABU
MANU	RUFARO
MASAMBA	SAWANDI
MAZI	SEKANI
MONGO	SIMBA
MUGO	TABARI
NAJJA	TWIA
NKOSI	YAKINI
OBA	ZAHUR
ODION	ZANI
OJO	ZUKA
OMARI	

He walked there now . . . thinking of names. Surely, he thought, he and his sister had some ancestor, some lithe young man with onyx skin and legs as straight as cane stalks, who had a name that was real. A name given to him at birth with love and seriousness. A name that was not a joke, nor a disguise, nor a brand name. But who this lithe young man was . . . could never be known. No. Nor his name.

—Toni Morrison, *Song of Solomon*

Wednesday Is Full of Woe

The Ashantis in West Africa name their children according to the day of the week on which they are born. Each day is believed to signify a certain temperament—for example, Monday boys are quiet and obedient, Wednesday boys fiery and aggressive. And sure enough, more offenses are committed by Wednesdays than by any others, with very few delinquents born on (and so named) Monday.

Names from across The ocean

Let's say your roots are Italian and you'd like to give your child a name that reflects your heritage, but want to go beyond names like Gino and Dino to find others that reflect the expressive beauty of the Italian language. What we offer here are mid-range choices from primarily European locales (for Anglo, Irish and Scottish names, see pp. 46–50; for African and Arabic names, see pp. 245–250; and for Hebrew names, see p. 229)—they have a distinctive ethnic flavor, yet are pleasing to the American ear.

FRENCH NAMES

G I R L S

ALAINE	ANGE
AMALIE	ARIANE
ANAIS	ARLETTE

AUBINE
BERTILLE
BLANCHETTE
CERISE
CHANTAL
CLAUDE
CLOTILDE
DELPHINE
ELIANE
ELODIE
FABIENNE
FLEUR
ISABEAU
JOELLE
LAURE

LEA
LEONIE
LIANNE
LUCIENNE
MANON
MAXIME
MIREILLE
MUSETTE
NICOLETTE
NOEMI
ODILE
SABINE
SOLANGE
SYLVIE
VIOLETTE

B O Y S

ALAIN
ARMAND
BARDIOU
BAUDIER
BENOIT
DIDIER
ETIENNE
FABIEN
FABRICE
GAUTIER
JULIEN

LAURENT
LUC
MATTHIEU
OLIVIER
PATRICE
RÉMI
TANGUY
THIBAULT
THIERRY
YVES

GERMAN NAMES

G I R L S

AMALIE	KATJA
ANJA	LORELEI
ANNALISE	MADY
ANTJE	MARTHE
BIRGITTE	MINA
CAROLA	MITZI
CONSTANZA	MONIKA
FREYA	PETRA
FRIDA	RENATE
FRITZI	SENTA
GRETE	TRESA
JAKOBINE	UTA
KARLOTTE	VERONIKE

B O Y S

ANDREAS	ESRA
ANSELM	GREGOR
ANTON	GÜNTER
ARNO	JUSTUS
AXEL	KASIMIR
BALTASR	KASPAR
BARTHEL	KONRAD
BRUNO	LAURENZ/LORENZ
CLAUDIUS	LUKAS
DIETRICH	MARKUS
DIX	MARIUS

MATHIAS
NIKLAS
THADDAUS

TOMAS
WERNER
WOLFGANG

GREEK NAMES

G I R L S

ACACIA
ACANTHA
ADELPHA
ALETHIA
ALPHA
ALYSIA
ANATOLA
ANEMONE
ANNIS
ANTHEA
APOLLINE
ASTA
ATHENA
CALANTHA
CALISTA
CALLA
CLIO
COSIMA
CYNARA
DAMARA
DORCAS
ELECTRA

ELENI
EUDOCIA
EULALIA
GAEA
KALLIOPE
KORA
KOREN
LALIA
LARISSA
MAIA
MELANTHA
NEOLA
NEOMA
NERISSA
ODESSA
OLYMPIA
PALLAS
PANTHEA
PHAIDRA
RHEA
SABA
STEFANIA

THADDEA	THEONE
THALASSA	ZELIA
THALIA	ZITA

B O Y S

ALEXANDROS	ILIAS
ANDREAS	KRISTIAN
ARTEMAS	LEANDER
BARNABAS	NEMO
CHRISTOS	NICODEMUS
CLAUDIOS	ORION
CONSTANTINE	PHILO
COSMO/KOSMOS	PLATO
CYPRIAN	STAVROS
DARIUS	VASILIS
HOMER	ZALE

ITALIAN NAMES

G I R L S

ADRIANA	EMILIA
ALLESSANDRA	FIORIANA
ALESSIA	GIANINA
ARIAN(N)A	GIOIA
CHIARA	GRAZIA
DOMENICA	ILARIA
DONATA	ISOTTA
ELETTRA	LIA
ELISABETTA	LIVIA

LUCIANA	RAFFAELLA
NOEMI	ROSALIA
ORIANA	SIMONA
OTTAVIA	VALERIA
PAOLINA	VIOLETTA
PIETRA	VIVIANA

B O Y S

ADRIANO	GUIDO
AMEDEO	LORENZO
BENEDETTO	LUCA
BRIANO	LUCIANO
CALVINO	MARCELLO
CLAUDIO	MARCO
CRISTIANO	MATTEO
DANTE	NUNZIO
DOMENICO	PAOLO
ELIO	PRIMO
EMILIO	RAFAELLO
ENZO	SILVIO
FABIANO	TADDEO
FEDERICO	UMBERTO
GIORDANO	VITTORIO
GIULIANO	

RUSSIAN, POLISH, AND OTHER SLAVIC NAMES

G I R L S

ALINA	KATINKA
ANASTASSIA	KATYA
ANIELA	KIRA
ANTONINA	LALA
ANYA	LARISA
CELINA	LILIANNA
DANICA	MASHA
EVELINA	NADIA
FANIA	NATALYA
FEDORA	OLGA
FEODORA	SASHA
FRANCISKA	TANIA
GALINA	TATIANA
ILONA	VARINA
IRINA	VARVARA
JANINA	VELIKA
JULESKA	VERUSHKA
KAMILLA	ZOFIA
KASSIA	

B O Y S

ALEXANDR	CASIMIR
ALEXI	DAVEED
ANATOL	DMITRI
ANDREI	DORJAN

FEODOR
IGOR
JANOS
JAREK
JENO
KASIMIR
LEV
MARIUS
MIKHAIL
NIKOLAI

ROMAN
SANDOR
SERGEI
TOMASZ
VASSILY
VLADIMIR
YURI
ZAREK
ZIV

SCANDINAVIAN NAMES

G I R L S

AINA
AMATA
ANNIKA
ASTA
ASTRID
BIRGET
DAGMAR
HANNA
KARIN

KRISTINA
LIV
MARTA
MARIT
REBEKKA
SONJA
TORIL
VALESKA
VIVECA/VIVEKA

B O Y S

ANDERS
ANDREAS
ARNE
AUDUN

BENEDIKT
BJÖRN
DAG
FINN

GUNNAR
GUNTHER
INGAR
IVAR
JENS
JORGEN
KNUT
LARS
LORENZ
LEIF
MARKUS
MORTEN

NELS
NILS
OLAF
PAAVO
SOREN
SKERRY
STIAN
SVEN
THOR
TOR
WRAY
ZAKARIAS

SPANISH NAMES

G I R L S

ADELINA
AIDA
ALEJANDRA
AMARA
ANA
ANICA
AQUILINA
CARMELA
CONSUELO
DALILA
DAVINA
DOMINGA
ESTRELLA
FABIANA

GRACIA
GUADALUPE
INES
JACINTA
LETICIA
LIANA
LUZ
MADALENA
MARISOL
MARQUITA
MERCEDES
MIGUELA
NELIA
PALOMA

PIA
PILAR
RAQUEL
SABANA
SARITA

SERAFINA
VIVIANA
YNES
YSABEL

B O Y S

ALEJANDRO
ALONSO
AMADEO
ARLO
CALVINO
CLAUDIO
CLEMENTE
CRISPO
DARIO
DIEGO
DOMINGO
ELVIO
EMILIO
ENRIQUE
ESTEBÁN
FABIO
FÉDERICO
FELIPE
FERNANDO
JAVIER
JEREMIAS
JOAQUIM
JORGE

LÁZARO
LEANDRO
LORENZO
LUCIO
MATEO
NALDO
ORLANDO
PABLO
PAZ
RAFAEL
RAÚL
REY
RICO
RUBÉN
RUFO
SEBÁSTIANO
TADEO
TAJO
TINO
TOMÁS
TULIO
YAGO

When I was a kid, I didn't know anybody named Heather or Joshua. In my neighborhood, boys had solid workmanlike names: Stanley, Chester, Walter, Norbert, Albert, Henry, or Joe. Girls had in-the-kitchen names like Bertha, Dorothy, Helen, Mildred, Eleanor, Mary, Lucille, and Gertrude.

But today, it's not unusual to find people with monikers like Heather Potkowski, Kevin Bongiorino, Danielle Goldberg. No wonder young people grow up confused about who they are.

—Mike Royko, *Chicago Tribune* syndicated column

INTO THE POOL

Some foreign-born celebs—most of them in the movies—have added their names to our national reservoir. Several of their names have gained widespread popularity, while others have seen only occasional use. The Names who have inspired these names include:

F E M A L E

ANOUK (b. Francoise)
Aimée
BIRGITTE Nielsen
BRIGITTE (b. Camille)
Bardot
BRITT Ekland
CHITA Rivera
CLAUDETTE Colbert
ELKE Sommer
GINA Lollobrigida
GLYNIS Johns
GREER Garson
GRETA Garbo
HAYLEY Mills
HEDY Lamarr
INGER Stevens
INGRID Bergman
ISABELLA Rosselini
IVANA Trump

KATARINA Witt
LILIA Skalia
LIV Ullmann
MARTINA Navratilova
MELINA Mercouri
MOIRA Shearer
NADIA Comaneci
NASTASSJA (b.
Natassja) Kinski
OLGA Korbut
ORIANNA Falacci
PAULINA Porizkova
PETULA Clark
SHEENA Easton
SIMONE Signoret
SINEAD O'Connor
SIOBHAN McKenna
SOPHIA Loren
VIVECA Lindfors

M A L E

ALAIN Delon
ALISTAIR Cooke
ARMAND Assante
BASIL Rathbone
BJÖRN Borg
CESAR Romero
DIRK Bogarde
DYLAN Thomas

ELIA Kazan
EMLYN Williams
ERROL Flynn
FABIO
FABRICE Morvan
(Milli Vanilli)
FERNANDO Lamas
INGMAR Bergman

JERZY Kozinski

MARCELLO
  Mastroianno

MIKHAIL Baryshnikov

MILOS Forman

NICOL Williamson

NOËL Coward

OMAR Sharif

PABLO Picasso

RAUL Julia

REX Harrison

RUTGER Hauer

SEAN Connery

TREVOR Howard

YVES Montand

ZUBIN Mehta

I think my name, Paloma, which means dove, is the most beautiful gift I was ever given. I never knew any other Palomas . . . and when you add it to Picasso, it's very striking and memorable, and that's good for business.

—Paloma Picasso quoted in *Lear's*

FAMILY TIES

YOU SAY MARIA, I SAY MARIAH; LET'S CALL THE WHOLE THING OFF

One of the few advantages of single parenthood must surely be that you get to choose your child's name all by yourself. When you become enchanted with Flora, there's no one around who will say, "Sounds like someone who sells violets in an alley." When you decide absolutely on Kevin, nobody pretends to gag, saying, "Forget it. I went to school with a Kevin who had bad breath." You don't have to deal with anyone wanting to name your child Rudolph after his great-grandfather or Sabra after the heroine of her favorite novel.

However, most people go into parenthood in pairs, and most couples choose their baby's name together. While having a child may, more than any other event, make you and your mate feel as one, choosing the child's name can highlight how separate you really are. Each of you brings your own associations, family history, ethnic background, taste, and imagination to the naming of a child. Attempting to merge all those elements and arrive at a name you both love can sometimes seem as futile as trying to predict your child's genetic makeup.

Some couples avoid wrangling over names by agreeing beforehand that one partner—usually the wife—will choose the children's names. Other husbands and wives split the selection process: He chooses the boys' names and she selects the girls', for instance, or she picks a name for the first child and he decides on the second. This sort of division of mental labor is usually found in couples who divide other kinds of decisions: He decides how to spend the money and she decides which laundry detergent to use, for example. In other words, it's old-fashioned.

Modern dads quite rightly expect an equal voice in choosing the name of the baby whose bottom they're going to diaper half the time, as do modern moms, who will be footing half the baby-sitter's salary. In addition, the fact that couples are marrying—and having children—later in life complicates the naming decision: The longer the separate "past" each partner has, the more potential for disagreement about names. In this case, names with happy old associations can be even more of a no-no than those with unpleasant ones. Resist the urge to commemorate that wonderful weekend you had in Capri five years ago with Carlo or Carlotta.

Some couples attempt to get a jump on the naming-decision process by beginning discussions long before they have a nine-month deadline, even before they have cemented their status as a couple. Names for potential children can become a symbolic turning point in a courtship. "My boyfriend says we can't even talk about getting married until

I agree to name our first son Bill," one woman told us. To him, Bill is the epitome of a good, solid name, like "My Boy Bill" in *Carousel;* to her, it's the retarded title character in the Mickey Rooney film. Wedding plans are still on hold.

Another couple, married for three months, takes long drives in the country to discuss names for their hypothetical child. "My husband likes the name Harry," says the woman. "Everybody in my family thinks it sounds really awful, like a janitor or something."

And a couple who argued about their son's name throughout the pregnancy were shocked in the delivery room by the arrival of a daughter. The husband's first words upon her birth: "Well, I guess that settles the Henry question." While it may have rendered moot their months-long argument over whether the name Henry sounded wimpy or strong, it introduced another question: what to name a girl.

Is there a way to sidestep all this angst in your search for a mutually satisfying name? Part of the solution lies in understanding the problem.

First, you should realize that issues such as differing associations with the names of family members, childhood friends and classmates, and past loves can never truly be resolved: If you went to school with a wonderful Tracy and your mate knew a terrible one, neither of you will ever be able to shake the association.

Differences in taste are stickier. You'll find that if you and your spouse tend to agree on style in clothes, furniture, music, and movies, you'll have an easier time agreeing on a name, or at least coming up with a group of names from which to choose. If, on the other hand, you're one of those couples who battle to the death over whether to buy an antique or a high-tech couch, you may be facing the same kind of fashion issue over choosing a name.

It helps to be aware that picking a name can uncover deep-seated issues of masculinity and femininity. A man may push for macho boys' names and ultrafeminine girls' names; a woman may push for ambisexual names for either. Obviously, what's at stake here is more than a name; it encompasses how you envision your son or daughter, and how you view the sexes in general.

How you see yourself vis à vis your own name can also breed disagreement between you and your mate. Growing up as a Ruth, say, may make you want to give your child a bouncy, fashionable name, while your husband, Jody, may wish to counter his own experience by choosing a name that's classic and grown-up.

While understanding all these problems may not make them go away, it can spark more enlightened naming discussions. Here are some concrete things you can do to arrive at a name that's an optimum choice for both of you:

Talk about issues like image and sexuality before you talk about names: What do you each hope for in a child? Is your fantasy child energetic or studious, "all-boy" or gentle, feminine or tomboy? Coming to agreement on these matters, or at least getting them out in the open, can help when you're choosing a name—not to mention raising your child.

Rule out all names of ex-girlfriends and ex-boyfriends. No matter how much you like the name Jill, do not proceed with it if your husband had a long, torrid affair with a Jill way back when. Do not tell yourself you'll forget: You won't, and neither will he.

Make a "no" list as well as a "yes" list: Most couples only make lists of the names they like; it can help to make lists, too, of the names that are absolutely out for each of you. Include those you'd rule out for personal reasons (the name of the guy who dumped you in high school and the roommate who stole all your clothes) as well as names you simply hate. Agree that neither of you will bring up the names on each other's "absolutely not" lists, no matter how much you like them or how neutral they may be for you.

Avoid using the name selection process as an opportunity to criticize each other's loved ones: When he campaigns for naming your son Morton after his father, this is not an excuse to tell him how much you hate his father, no matter how much you hate the name Morton. Surely you can find enough negative things to say about the name itself without widening the battlefield.

Investigate the reasons for each other's choices: Let's say you love a name your spouse hates. Instead of fighting over the name itself, explore what it is about the name that appeals to you. Figuring out whether you like a name because it's classic, or feminine, or stylish, say, can lead you to other names with the same characteristics that you both may like.

Remember that parenthood is a joint venture: Just as your child will be a unique blend of characteristics from both of you, so should you endeavor to arrive at a name that combines each of your sensibilities and tastes. It will take some enlightened thinking, searching, and negotiating, but that's what this book is all about.

PUTTING THE NAME BEFORE THE BABY

In this age of amniocentesis and ultrasound, many parents have the option of knowing their baby's sex—and thus making a firm decision on a name—long before his or her arrival.

While these medical advances have been a boon for mothers and babies alike, and knowing your child's sex can cut the work of choosing a name in half, we nevertheless caution against telling the world your child's gender and name months before his or her actual arrival.

Announcing in mid-pregnancy that a boy named Dawson is waiting to be born can have a dampening effect on his entrance into the world. For one thing, other people tend to draw a more or less complete picture of little Dawson's looks and personality, based on his name and their knowledge of his parents, long before they get a chance to meet him! For another, you may find that other people are actually less eager to meet him. Instead of waiting by the phone for news of your baby's sex and name, they may receive your announcement with a bored, "Oh, Dawson's finally here."

The only real advantage we can cite for sharing your child's name before his birth is not really that much of a plus: People can give you shower gifts of little T-shirts with Dawson spelled out on the back.

BAD ADVICE?

What are you going to name the baby?

That's the question of the hour, or rather, the question of the entire nine months leading up to your baby's birth.

Everyone from your family and friends to the woman selling newspapers at the corner will want to know. The problem is that all those people will have opinions, too—contradictory, confusing, often debilitating.

Let's say you and your mate have agreed that, if the baby is a boy, you will name him Ned. You tell your mother-in-law.

"I had a great-uncle Ned," she says. Pause. "He was a drunk."

You tell your best friend.

"Have you noticed," she says, "how so many nerdy movie characters are called Ned?"

You tell your brother.

"Sounds like a seventy-year-old," he says.

You tell your ten-year-old, who makes gagging noises. "All the kids will hate him!" she cries.

Your four-year-old agrees with his sister. "I hate him," he says.

Before all these outside opinions, you thought Ned was a fine name; now you're not so sure. And even if you still like the name Ned, you don't want your child's grandmother to associate him with the family alcoholic, your friends to gossip about how bad your taste is, or your other children to reject the baby because of his name.

So you and your husband come up with a new idea. Let's say it's Jack. This time, your mother-in-law approves, your best friend thinks it's too groovy, your brother thinks it's bland, and your kids still hate it.

All right: How about Omar? Your mother-in-law, brother, and best friend all think it's too bizarre; the ten-year-old thinks it's cool; the four-year-old stands fast in his dislike.

At this point, you may be catching on to the fact that

the four-year-old might be having problems with the idea of the baby beyond choosing its name. And it also might be dawning on you that, no matter what name you set forth, there's going to be someone who doesn't like it. How do you decide which naming advice you take to heart, which you disregard?

The first step might be to consider your sources. People who've never had kids may be ignorant of swings in style and may also be out of touch with how names affect kids. Other children in your family may have a very good idea of how a name will be perceived by fifth graders, but no long-range take on a name's viability. A friend or relative who's had children in the past five years, on the other hand, may be able to give you an educated opinion on a name's popularity as well as advise you on how the choice of a name feels to a parent over time.

The next step may be to review the general taste of those offering their opinions. Would you let these people choose what color you paint your house? Would you let them pick out your clothes? Their tastes in other matters are a good indication of the validity of their taste in names.

The final step—which often proves to be very enlightening—is to ask those who offer opinions for name suggestions of their own. You may very well find that your mother-in-law loves the name John, too basic for your tastes. Your best friend suggests Homer and Jethro, which you find too offbeat. Your brother likes Darryl and Curtis, too declassé. The ten-year-old offers Max and Sam, the names of the most popular boys in her class, but too popular for you. And the four-year-old's idea of a good name? Rainbow Boy.

Despite all those negative opinions, you may find Ned sounds better by the minute.

In Search of a Girl's Name

. . . Jane stroked the pale brown down on the baby's head. "What does she look like to you? She looks like a Miranda to me."

"No."

"No."

"Samantha? Christiana?"

"No exotic names."

"Those aren't exotic. How about Gwendolyn?"

"How about Mary?"

"Are you serious, Nick? . . . Mary Cobleigh. It sounds like a barmaid. But Maria might not be bad . . ."

"Too Catholic. . . ."

"How about Tuttle? . . ."

"I hate that," Nicholas said. "I keep meeting all these girls named Heywood and Lockhart and they always had dumb-bunny nicknames. Although . . . I sort of like Heissenhuber Cobleigh. It has a distinguished ring to it. A fine old name. A noble—"

"If you don't stop I'll put Tammy on the birth certificate."

"I've got it, Jane!"

"This should be terrific."

"Dorothy."

"Even John would be better than that. . . ."

"Come on, now. We need a nice, plain, pretty name. Caroline."

"It sounds like we're copying the Kennedys."

"All right. Ann."

". . . A little too simple. Even with an e."

"Elizabeth."

"I like that," Jane said. "But . . . she doesn't look like an Elizabeth."

"If you name her Zelda then she'll look like a Zelda."

"No, she won't. . . . Let me think. Olivia and Abigail are out. And Winifred. . . . I know," Jane said. "Victoria."

"Victoria?"

"Victoria Cobleigh. It's a little regal, but that's okay. . . . What do you think?"

"You're not going to call her Tory, are you?"

"No! Maybe Vicky, if she's athletic and energetic like you. But otherwise just beautiful, elegant, gorgeous, adorable, sweet, cuddly—"

"Victoria."

—Susan Isaacs, *Almost Paradise*

BABY, JR.

The easiest solution to the question of what to name a baby boy is to simply repeat the father's name, appending to it the letters Jr. Although this practice is fading out of fashion, it does have certain advantages: a direct link with a progenitor, the pride that goes with carrying on a family name.

But the disadvantages can outweigh the benefits. The child may well feel he's inheriting an identity along with a name, that he's merely a paler shadow of his father, that he will always be number two.

If a boy is actually addressed by the same name as his father, countless confusions will arise, from the most obvious, such as "Which Donald do you want, Big Donald or Little Donald?" on the phone, and fathers and sons opening (and reading) each other's mail, to more subtle ones, like mother having to call the two most important males in her life, husband and son, by the same name.

On the other hand, if the child is called Junior, he is somewhat dehumanized, almost like being referred to as a number, and a lesser number than his father at that. More common is for the child to be known by a familiar, childish form of the name, a practice that spawns its own perils. Dad is Don and junior is Donny, forever locked by his name into an adolescent (or younger) image of himself that persists long after he leaves home. Or, even worse, he might be known to the world as Bud, Buster, Butch, Sonny, Skip, or Chip.

Giving a boy the same name as his father and grandfather—making him a III—is a somewhat different issue. On the positive side, it could be argued that you're carrying on a family tradition rather than purely indulging in egotism. And honorable WASP nicknames for IIIs—Tripp, Tre, or Trey—are not quite as humiliating as the ones many juniors are saddled with. On the down side, little Frederick or Albert the third has the image of not one but two grown-up men to live up to, with a fairly strong (and potentially overwhelming) mandate to carry on the family tradition.

Only one president in the history of the United States has been a junior—James Earl Carter, Jr., who, as we all know, insisted on being known by his childhood nickname of Jimmy. Gerald Ford was born Leslie Lynch King, Jr., but his name was changed when he was adopted by his stepfather. Vice President Albert Gore is a junior, and the man we know as Bill Clinton was born William Jefferson Blythe IV. Relatively few juniors are to be found among high achievers in sports or the fine arts. However, there are lots of military men, junior grade.

How to avoid the pitfalls of juniordom and still name your son after his father? You could go the royal route and name him Donald Dalton Duckworth II. Or the child could be given a different middle name, say Donald Duncan Duckworth, be called Duncan by the family, and later sign his memos D. Duncan Duckworth. But before taking this approach, remember the old saying, "Don't trust anyone who parts his name on the side."

Some juniors who made names for themselves

KAREEM ABDUL-JABBAR (Ferdinand Lewis Alcindor, Jr.)
EDWARD ALBERT, Jr.
MUHAMMAD ALI (Cassius Marcellus Clay, Jr.)
ARTHUR ASHE, Jr.
ED BEGLEY, Jr.
HARRY BELAFONTE (Harold George Belafonte, Jr.)
SEN. JOE BIDEN (Joseph Robinette Biden, Jr.)
MARLON BRANDO, Jr.
LLOYD BRIDGES (Lloyd Vernet Bridges, Jr.)
YUL BRYNNER (Taidje Khan, Jr.)

WILLIAM F. BUCKLEY, Jr.
LEVAR BURTON (Le Vardis Robert Martyn Burton, Jr.)
JAMES CAGNEY (James Francis Cagney, Jr.)
JIMMY CARTER (James Earl Carter, Jr.)
RAYMOND CARVER (Raymond Clevey Carver, Jr.)
LON CHANEY, Jr.
CHUBBY CHECKER (Ernest Evans, Jr.)
THOMAS L. CLANCY, Jr.
VAN CLIBURN (Harvey Lavan Cliburn, Jr.)
HARRY CONNICK, Jr.
JIMMY CONNORS (James Scott Connors, Jr.)
JACKIE COOPER (John Cooper, Jr.)
BILL COSBY (William H. Cosby, Jr.)
HUME CRONYN (Hume Blake, Jr.)
WALTER CRONKITE (Walter Leland Cronkite, Jr.)
ROBERT DE NIRO, Jr.
JOHN DENVER (Henry John Deutschendorf, Jr.)
TROY DONAHUE (Merle Johnson, Jr.)
MORTON DOWNEY, Jr.
ROBERT DOWNEY, Jr.
CLINT EASTWOOD (Clinton Eastwood, Jr.)
BUDDY EBSEN (Christian Rudolf Ebsen, Jr.)
DOUGLAS FAIRBANKS, Jr. (Douglas Elton Thomas
    Ullman, Jr.)
ALBERT FINNEY, Jr.
CUBA GOODING, Jr.
BERRY GORDY, Jr.
ALBERT GORE, Jr.
LOUIS GOSSETT, Jr.
ALEXANDER M. HAIG, Jr.
HAL HOLBROOK (Harold Rowe Holbrook, Jr.)
WILLIAM HOLDEN (William Franklin Beedle, Jr.)

ROCK HUDSON (Roy Harold Scherer, Jr.)
HUBERT HORATIO HUMPHREY, Jr.
HENRY JAMES, Jr.
QUINCY JONES, Jr.
STACY KEACH (Walter Stacy Keach, Jr.)
BUSTER KEATON (Joseph Francis Keaton, Jr.)
MARTIN LUTHER KING, Jr.
ELMORE JOHN LEONARD, Jr.
RALPH MACCHIO, Jr.
OLIVER NORTH (Oliver Laurence North, Jr.)
ADAM CLAYTON POWELL, Jr.
RONALD REAGAN, Jr.
ROBERT REDFORD (Charles Robert Redford, Jr.)
BURT REYNOLDS (Burton Leon Reynolds, Jr.)
CAL RIPKEN, Jr.
JASON ROBARDS, Jr.
SMOKEY ROBINSON (William Robinson, Jr.)
MICKEY ROONEY (Joe Yule, Jr.)
MICKEY ROURKE (Philip André Rourke, Jr.)
RIP TORN (Elmore Torn, Jr.)
KURT VONNEGUT, Jr.
ROBERT WAGNER, Jr.
HANK WILLIAMS, Jr.
TOM WOLFE (Thomas Kennerly Wolfe, Jr.)
FRANK ZAPPA (Francis Vincent Zappa, Jr.)
EFREM ZIMBALIST, Jr.

EDWARD ALBEE (Edward Franklin Albee III)
ALEC BALDWIN (Alexander Rae Baldwin III)
BEAU BRIDGES (Lloyd Vernet Bridges III)
TOM CRUISE (Thomas Cruise Mapother IV)

OSCAR HAMMERSTEIN II
OREL HERSCHEISER (Orel Leonard Herscheiser IV)
LEE MAJORS (Harvey Lee Yeary II)
JACK LEMMON (John Uhler Lemmon III)
TRINI LOPEZ (Trinidad Lopez III)
LUKE PERRY (Coy Luther Perry III)
CLIFF ROBERTSON (Clifford Parker Robertson III)
TOM SMOTHERS (Thomas Bolyn Smothers III)
LOUDON WAINWRIGHT III
CLARENCE WILLIAMS III

Junior spacemen

Although it isn't a written requirement, being a junior certainly seems to help one's chances of getting into the space program. Juniors who have been launched include:

EDWIN E. ALDRIN, Jr.
CHARLES BASSETT II
GUION S. BLUFORD, Jr.
CHARLES F. BOLDEN, Jr.
ROY D. BRIDGES, Jr.
CHARLES CONRAD, Jr.
L. GORDON COOPER, Jr.
CHARLES M. DUKE, Jr.
JOHN H. GLENN, Jr.
RICHARD F. GORDON, Jr.
FRED W. HAISE, Jr.
HENRY W. HARTSFIELD, Jr.
ROBERT H. LAWRENCE, Jr.
JAMES A. LOVELL, Jr.

THOMAS K. MATTINGLY II
ELLIOT SEE, Jr.
WALTER M. SCHIRRA, Jr.
BREWSTER H. SHAW, Jr.
ALAN B. SHEPARD, Jr.
JOHN L. SWIGART, Jr.
EDWARD H. WHITE II

. . . In the world of juniors, I was one of the lucky ones. I was never called "Junior" as a nickname. I knew one Junior for years without ever knowing his real name. He and other Juniors will tell you that Junior is their real name and sign it that way on a greeting card or a letter. These are the guys people probably have in mind when they ask me if I have a fragile sense of identity because of my juniorhood. . . . I think that when I was named for my father, the intention was that my name not be simply a utile thing, not be just a handy sound to summon a boy when the garbage needs to be taken down. When a child is named, it is an attempt to define the child. And my definition is my father. I thank my parents for their vote of confidence and I hope I live up to my name. . . .

—Rafael A. Suarez, Jr., "Being a Jr.,"
The New York Times Magazine

Henry James disliked his junior status in-
tensely—"I have a right to speak of that ap-
pendage—I carried it about for forty years . . .
disliking it all the while, and with my dislike
never in the least understood or my state pitied."

—Leon Edel, *Henry James, the Untried Years*

George V isn't just a dead king of England and
a tony Paris hotel—he's also George Foreman's
infant son. In a move Gertrude Stein might have
applauded, the heavyweight contender dubbed
his new baby George V: he joins three older
brothers, George II, III and IV. . . . "We're
gonna call this one Red" [Foremon said], "because you know what green means—keep going."

—*Newsweek*

SIBLING NAMES
(FOR FIRST-TIME PARENTS ALSO)

If you're having your second, third, fourth child or beyond, you have probably already experienced the inherent difficulties and dilemmas involving sibling names. Ideally, the names you choose for later children should "go with" the name you picked for your first child: They should be harmonious in rhythm and style. At the same time, names of later children should be different enough from the first child's name to avoid confusion. Yes, there are families with a Jane and a Jean, a Larry and a Harry, an Ellen and an Eleanor, but the resulting mix-ups do not seem worth the cuteness.

The real problem with sibling names arises because most parents don't consider later names when they choose the first. But the first choice sets the pattern, narrowing future options. Here's how it works:

Because we have personal experience with this one, let's say you decided to name your first child, a girl, Rory. Good enough, but now you're about to have your second. Names that rhyme are out: Goodbye Laurie, Corey, Glory, Maury, Tory, et al. So too with similar-sounding names: everything in the Rose family, the Mary family, the Doria group, the Lauras, Coras, Noras, and Floras, not to mention Larry, Gerry, Terry; Rowen, Rourke, Rollo. You get the idea.

Also, because Rory is such a distinctively Celtic name, it would sound odd with a name from a different ethnic background. Rory and Francesca won't do, for example. In terms of image, Rory is clearly a High-Energy name. Would it be fair to pair her name with one from the Intellectual Power group? Would a little sister named Ruth, for example, always feel bookwormish by contrast; would Rory, conversely, feel flighty in comparison? Another consideration is the name's ambisexuality. Choosing a sister's name from the Feminine or Feminissima group—Angelica, for instance, or Melissa—might not only sound discordant but could make the two girls feel differently about their sexuality. And if the sibling is a boy, giving him an ambisexual name could make matters even more confusing. A girl named Rory with a brother named Ashley? It just wouldn't work. Finally, Rory is a somewhat unusual name, and a more classic choice for a brother or sister could also strike the wrong chord. Rory and Jane? Rory and John? Somehow, they just don't belong together.

Further complications set in if you have changed your ideas about names after living with your real live first choice for a few years. You may regret choosing an ambisexual name like Rory because of the confusion over whether the child was a boy or a girl, and may also wish you had chosen a more common name that was easier for the child to pronounce and for others to understand. You may really want to name your second child Jane or John, and yet not feel comfortable with those choices.

The point of all this is to encourage you to consider future possibilities when you're choosing the name of your first child. If your two favorite names are Anna and Hannah, for example, realize that picking one now rules out the other forever. When you're deciding among several names, consider the future implications of each. Imagining which names might follow for other children may help you narrow the field.

What, in particular, works and what doesn't? Without taste or value judgments on the specific names, we can tell you some instances of sibling names we're familiar with that do work. Jane and William, for instance, or Sam and Lily. Both pairings are good because, for one, the girls' names are clearly feminine and the boys' clearly masculine. The style is consistent: fashionable, but not to the point of cliché. And the names sound well together but do not sound confusingly alike. Another good brother-and-sister combo is Elizabeth and Charles, called Libby and Charley. Both are classic names that happen to be in style now, and both nicknames are gently old-fashioned, more compatible than, say, Liza and Chuck would be.

Two brothers whose names catch the right rhythm are Felix and Leo. Both are traditional names—saints' names in fact—that, because they hadn't been widely used for some years, have an appealingly offbeat quality. The *x* and the *o* endings provide different but equally unusual sounds for the two names, and they are further related by both being feline.

We know a family of three girls named Melissa, Danielle, and Lauren. Their mother wanted to name the third daughter Patricia. But the classic Patricia—or Pat or Patti—simply did not sound like the sister of the trendier Melissa and Danielle, so Lauren she became.

When the name of a fictional character breaks rank with those of his or her siblings, there's usually some symbolism involved. The classic case is *Little Women*'s Meg, Jo, Beth, and Amy. Even if you haven't read the book, guess which one was the tomboy with ambitions greater than her sisters'.

So too in real life, where the child with a name that is "different" from those of his brothers and sisters may also feel different in spirit. We know of a family with four children named Mary, Christopher, Nicole, and Alexandra. It's clear here too which one considers herself the odd child out.

If you already have your first child and are choosing a name for a sibling, keep the following guidelines in mind:

Don't be cute: No rhymes, sound plays, precious pairings. Resist the temptation, for example to name Daisy's sister Maisie, Darcy, or Hyacinth.

Don't fall into the same initial trap: A trend of the fifties and sixties was to choose sibling names all starting with the same letter. Sometimes, parents didn't consider the consequences if they had chosen to start with the letter E and happened to have, say, five boys. Edward was fine for the first, Eliot okay for the second, but by the birth of their fifth son they were stuck with choices like Earl, Elmer, and Egbert. While few parents have five children today, the same-initial trend should be avoided as dated and overly precious.

Do maintain consistency of style, image, sex, and tradition: This rule is to be interpreted loosely, but, as detailed in the example of Rory, sibling names should ideally stay in the same, well, family.

Be careful about sexual distinctions: If you choose a boyish name for your daughter, and later have a son, go with a boy's name that is clearly masculine. So too if you give your boy an ambisexual name; both he and his little sister will fare better if her name is distinctly feminine. The names of same-sex children should not have widely divergent sexual images: Bruno's brother shouldn't be named Blair, for instance, nor should Belinda's sister.

Avoid using two names with the same nickname: This problem usually crops up when parents, hoping for a junior, despair at the third girl and name her Roberta or Christina or Geraldine. She then becomes Bobbie or Chris or Gerry. When

her long-awaited little brother is born five years later, he is
named Robert or Christopher or Gerald. Try as the parents
might to prevent it, they may end up with a Bobbie and a
Bobby, Chris and Chris, or Gerry and Gerry, in addition, of
course, to Bobby, Chris, or Gerry Sr. The trend toward
smaller families has headed off most occurrences of this problem in recent years, but it still happens. If you're entirely
positive that if you ever have a boy you'll name him Christopher, don't name a girl Christina when you give up hope
on having a son, or vice versa. Accidents do happen.

Double trouble

Twins offer a rare opportunity for parents to choose two related
names at the same time, but also multiply the difficulties inherent
in sibling names. With twins, it can be more tempting to use
rhyme, sound play, and same-initial names, but in our opinion
pairings like Eddie and Teddy, Faith and Charity, or Charles and
Charlene should be relegated to a time capsule. While same-
initial names that are clearly distinct from one another, such as
Ross and Rachel, twin children of Jane Pauley and Garry Trudeau, are okay, different-initial names that are consistent in style
and tone are preferable.

Some celebrity examples that work: Cybill Shepherd's
Ariel and Zack; Denzel Washington's Malcolm and Olyvia;
Ron Howard's Paige and Jocelyn. In all these cases, the names
are distinct from each other yet make a harmonious pair—
exactly what most parents would want for the twins themselves.

Two examples of twin names that don't work—Debby
Boone's Gabrielle and Dustin, and Mia Farrow and André
Previn's Matthew and Sascha—fall short for the same reason:

Each set has one sexually distinct name and one ambi name. Based on the names alone, one would surmise that they were both boy-girl pairs. In fact, Gabrielle and Dustin are twin girls, and Matthew and Sascha are both boys.

Whatever the sex of the children, twin names should present a compatible image. As detailed in the discussion on sibling names, pairings like Gigi and Walter or Candida and Jennifer are too discordant. Gigi's twin would better be named, perhaps, Barnaby; Walter's sister might be Margaret; Candida's twin could conceivably be called Isabella; and Jennifer's obvious other half is—who else?—Jason.

WHOSE NAME IS IT, ANYWAY?

It is Thanksgiving. You and your sister-in-law, both newly pregnant, are sitting with the rest of the family around the table. Talk turns to names.

"If we have a boy, of course he will be Richard the Third," says your sister-in-law, smiling sweetly at your father. Your brother, Richard Jr., beams.

You, on the other hand, choke on your cranberry sauce. Ever since you were a little girl, you've wanted to name your first son Richard. Besides being your father's name, it's also your husband's father's name, your brother's name, and your favorite boy's name in all the world.

"We were planning on Richard, too," you manage to sputter.

"You can't have it," booms your brother. "Clearly it's our name."

"There's room for two Richards in the family," you reason. "We'll just use different nicknames."

"That's stupid," your brother says. "Ricky and Richie?"

"Now, now," soothes your mother. "What if you have girls?"

"Amanda," you and your brother say in unison.

If you and your spouse have proliferating siblings, the issue of who gets to use which names is one you may have to face. And a difficult issue it is. Does a son have absolute dibs on the father's name? Is there room in a family for two cousins with the same name? Is there a pecking order for who gets traditional family names? Is getting there first a good enough reason to usurp somebody else's name? Can you set claims on a name to begin with?

How you answer these questions depends a lot on your individual family. In some families, the oldest son has eternal right to his father's name, even if he never has a son of his own. In others, it's first come, first served, with the understanding that there will be no later duplications. And some families just play catch-as-catch-can, and worry later about how they'll deal with three cousins named, say, Eric.

If you anticipate some name-wrestling within your own family, keep the following tips in mind:

Announce your choices early on: If you have an absolute favorite name you're sure you will use, don't make a secret of it. Planting it in everyone's mind as "your" name can help avoid problems later.

Don't steal someone else's name: We're not talking about naming your baby Letitia, unaware that, on the same day in a different state, your sister is naming her baby Letitia. We're talking about naming your baby Letitia when your sister has been saying since she was fifteen that her fondest wish in life was to have a little girl named Letitia. And your sister is eight months pregnant. And knows she's having a girl.

Avoid carbon copies: Two little Caroline Townsend Smiths in a close-knit family is one too many. If you want to use the same first and middle names that a sibling uses, can you live with a different nickname—Carrie, for instance? Or can you vary the middle name, so that, at least within the family, one cousin is called Caroline Townsend and the other, say, Caroline Louise? The only case in which two cousins named Caroline Townsend and called Caroline can work is if they have different last names.

Honor family traditions: If the oldest child of the oldest child in your family is always named Taylor, don't break rank, unless your oldest sibling is a nun, priest, or Gay Rights organizer and formally renounces rights to the name.

Take unintentional, unimportant duplications in stride: We know two sisters-in-law, living across the country from each other, who were pregnant at the same time: Jane due in January and Anne in April. During their annual Christmas Eve phone conversation, Jane said she was sure she'd have a boy, and that they were planning to name him Edward. "That's our name," gasped Anne. "Too bad," Jane said blithely. After a few minutes of intense anxiety, Anne decided Jane was right. Neither had officially "claimed" Edward, nor was it a name with any family significance. It would be as ridiculous to insist that Jane change her choice at the eleventh hour as it would be to deny her own son the name just so it wouldn't duplicate that of a cousin he'd see, at best, once a year. Besides, Jane favored the nickname Eddie, while Anne preferred Ted. P.S.: Due to mitigating circumstances, neither baby was named Edward. They ended up Juliet and Josephine.

NAME IN THE MIDDLE

What of your child's middle name?

The strongest trend today is to give your baby a middle name that has meaning. It might be your maiden name, another family surname, the name of someone close to you, or a name with more personal symbolic meaning. Many first-born sons who are not juniors are still given their fathers' names as middle names; increasingly, daughters are getting their mothers' first names as middle names.

Another trend, sparked by the new generation of royal babies, is to give your child more than one middle name, à la little Prince William Arthur Philip Louis, to honor all the relatives in one fell swoop.

You may want to balance an unusual first name with a more solid middle name, or vice versa, if you're unsure of your choice and want to give your child an option later. Or perhaps you feel obligated by tradition or family pressure to give your child a name you absolutely hate: Its place is tucked discreetly in the middle.

Still another increasingly popular option is to give your child no middle name at all. A growing number of parents feel that unless a middle name has some personal meaning, it serves no purpose and may border on the pretentious; others feel that a middle name is "wasted" on a girl, who may drop it when she marries, slotting her maiden name in the middle. (With more and more women keeping their original last names after marriage, this argument no longer stands up.)

What is decidedly out of fashion is giving your child a "throwaway" middle name—a euphonic if insignificant bridge between the first and last name. These are the Anns, Sues, and Lees of our childhoods, names that no one particularly liked or cared about, but that sounded right to the fifties ear following Lisa or Barbara or Karen. The single exception to this is the middle name Rose, see page 10.

Even more passé (except in the South, where the practice has always been beyond fashion) is giving your child a throwaway middle name you don't throw away—naming her Lisa Ann, for instance, and calling her Lisa Ann.

Do you know where we went wrong? We named 'em. That's when you get all attached.

—Roseanne

THE NAME BECOMES THE CHILD

Finally comes the day when you hold your live child in your arms and make a final decision on a real live name. At that point, all the lists you've made, the considerations you've weighed, and the options you've juggled fall by the wayside and you and your child are left with your ultimate choice.

What happens then?

Well, on one hand, the struggle over Miranda vs. Molly seems less crucial in the face of three A.M. feedings, colic, and the high cost of diapers. And it doesn't take very long for your baby's persona to dominate the name, for your baby to become his or her name. For the first two weeks, you may find yourself still calling little Miranda "It"; for the next few, you may feel self-conscious each time you pronounce the name; but a month later you'll find that when you say "Miranda" you don't hear the sound of the name but see instead your child's curved lips and dark curls.

On the other hand, once you've settled on a name, you deal with its myriad implications, often for the first time. You may discover, for instance, that your Aunt Elizabeth is not satisfied to be honored by a mere middle name, that people on the street do not necessarily assume Jordan is a girl, and that friends have to suppress a snicker when you tell them you've named your son Henry.

This may not be fun. This may cause you to retrieve your original lists of possibilities and say to your spouse in the middle of the night, "Maybe we should have named him Michael." And of course, it is possible to change a child's name two days or two months or even two years after you've given it, but it's not easy for many reasons and it's not what we're considering here.

Better than contemplating a name change would be to mull over the fact that choosing one option—in names as in everything else—always means forgoing all others. That the name you've selected inevitably becomes influenced by reality, while the ones you've rejected remain fantasies, entirely pleasant because you alone control them. That in fact if you had chosen Michael, say, you might then be worrying about its ordinariness, might be wishing in the middle of the night that you had gone with something more distinctive like . . . Henry.

Obviously, much of the value of this book is that it helps you anticipate the real world repercussions of a name. And much of the impetus for writing it came from our own experiences and those of our friends in choosing names for children and living with the choices.

One of our friends, for instance, has two children: Emily and Jeremy. "When Emily was born we were living in the country and it seemed like a really special, unusual name," she says. "Then when she was a few months old we moved to the city and I discovered that there were little Emilys everywhere. I felt terrible. I would listen in the playground for other kids named Emily, I would pore over nursery school class lists for other Emilys, and if she was the only Emily I'd feel so relieved. On one hand I feel badly because it seems as if the name is a cliché, but there also aren't so many Emilys as I'd originally feared."

Our friend pinpoints another reason why she was unaware of how widely used the name Emily was (and another reason we wrote this book): "Having a first child I didn't really know any other young parents. I had no idea what people were talking about when they named their kids or what the new style was. My idea of a trendy name was still Barbara or Sue."

What then of Jeremy's name? "That one I haven't had so many problems with," she says, "except that some people keep trying to call him Jerry."

Parents who've chosen less usual names talk of unanticipated problems with pronunciation and comprehension. A little girl named Leigh is sometimes called "Lay"; a child named Hannah is called Anna by some people. One of us has some regrets about calling her daughter Rory because the name is more often understood as Laurie, Corey, Tory, Dory, or even Gloria or Marie than as its rightful self.

Then there's the issue of the child's name vis à vis his or her looks and personality. Many parents wait to make a name choice until they see which of their finalists best fits the child. This makes some sense, but you should be aware that a newborn is not necessarily representative of the five- or twelve-year-old he or she will become. The chubby, noisy infant daughter you name Casey may grow into a dainty, ultrafeminine ballet dancer, while the delicate baby who seems to be the quintessential Arabella may become, ten years later, goalie on the neighborhood boys' hockey team.

This brings us to the flip side of this issue: Children can irrevocably color our perceptions of their names. You undoubtedly have unique feelings about certain names based on the children you know who bear them, and so do we. When we disagreed about whether to include a particular name on a list here, it was usually because we each knew people who brought different things to it: a handsome and irreverent Ralph, for example, vs. a boorish one; an adorable kid named Kermit vs. the frog on TV.

Reading this book can help prepare you for some of a name's eventualities, then, but not for others. You wouldn't be surprised, as our friend was, that Emily is a fashionable name or that some people are bent on using undesirable nicknames. Neither will you be unaware of both the advantages and the complications of giving your child a popular or an unusual name, or that Cameron can also be a girl's name, or that Henry has an intellectual image and so can be perceived by some people as a bit nerdy.

But no one, including you, has ultimate control over the person your child turns out to be. A name can remind you of your hopes and fears way back when childbirth was a point on the horizon, but your child—the one who's laughing or crawling or walking across the room in his own special way—can remind you that Henry by any other name, be it Michael or Melchizedek, would still be your own sweet boy.

INDEX

GIRLS' NAMES

Aphrodite, 143
Apolline, 255
Apollonia, 237
April, 121, 161, 202
Aprili, 248
Aquilina, 237, 260
Ara, 245
Arabella, 26, 43, 111, 158, 225
Araminta, 47, 161
Arbella, 225
Ardith, 111
Aretha, 82
Ariadne, 106, 107, 111, 237
Ariana, 158, 256
Ariane, 46, 115, 252
Arianna, 256
Ariel, 22, 90, 96, 111, 122, 158,
   232, 286
Arielle, 232
Arissa, 68
Arlene, 56, 202, 203
Arletta, 161
Arlette, 252
Ashira, 232
Ashley, xvii, 14, 22, 26, 60, 65, 68,
   75, 78, 89, 90, 122, 140, 154,
   169, 190, 209, 210, 283
Ashling, 50
Asia, 17, 207
Assisi, 17
Asta, 255, 259
Astra, 111
Astrid, 43, 259
Athena, 255
Atlanta, 18
Aubine, 253
Aubrey, 40
Audra, 111, 161
Audrey, 11, 56, 161, 203, 237
Augusta, 33, 225
Aura, 115
Aurelia, 43, 111
Auria, 237
Aurora, 111, 158
Ava, 237
Aveline, 225
Avery, 6, 14, 26
Avigail, 232

Avis, 33
Aviva, 232
Avivah, 232
Avril, 48
Ayasha, 245
Ayn, 82
Aza, 245
Aziza, 232, 248

Bab, 220
Babby, 220
Babe, 144, 220
Babette, 158, 220
Babs, 220
Bailey, 14, 191
Bambi, 121, 144, 147
Baraka, 248
Barakah, 245
Barb, 220
Barbara, 25, 56, 65, 149, 166, 202,
   215, 220, 293
Barbie, 85, 117, 144, 158, 220
Barbra, 86
Barnaby, 40
Barra, 111
Barrie, 168, 169
Basil, 40
Bathoc, 227
Bathsheba, 234
Bathsira, 245
Batsheva, 234
Bean, 70
Beatrice, 96, 108, 141, 161, 225, 237
Beatrix, 11, 48, 161, 237
Becca, 161
Becky, 208
Belinda, 158, 285
Belle, 36, 68, 161
Belva, 33
Benita, 161
Berenice, 225
Beril, 115
Bernadette, 33, 81, 131, 141, 161
Bernice, 56, 108, 166
Berry, 169
Bertha, 32, 135, 166, 262
Bertille, 253
Beryl, 169

BOYS' NAMES